Title: "Unveiling the Self and Spirit: Embracing the Shadows"

By Vlad Orfeo

Old Ways of the Soul

Vlad Orfeo

INTRUDUCTION

In the depths of every human heart lies a mysterious realm, concealed from the light of consciousness - the domain of shadows. These hidden aspects of ourselves, often ignored or denied, hold the key to profound self-discovery and transformation. Welcome to a journey of inner exploration, as we embark on the path of Shadow Work.

Life's tapestry weaves together both light and darkness, joy and sorrow, triumphs and tribulations. Our experiences shape us, molding the multifaceted individuals we become. However, not all facets of ourselves are easily embraced, for some dwell within the shadows. The concept of "Shadow Work" is not a mystical art or a hidden secret; rather, it is a profound and courageous endeavor to acknowledge and integrate the parts of ourselves we might rather keep hidden or avoid altogether.

Through centuries, sages, shamans, and philosophers alike have recognized the significance of understanding and addressing these shadowy aspects. Carl Jung, the renowned Swiss psychiatrist, illuminated the path for modern explorers of the psyche, emphasizing the importance of "making the unconscious conscious." In doing so, we come to understand that the shadows contain not just darkness but hidden potential and untapped wisdom.

In this book, we will journey together into the heart of shadow work, delving into its principles, methods, and transformative power. We shall face our fears, heal past wounds, and embrace our hidden gifts, emerging stronger and more integrated beings. The path may be challenging, but the rewards are boundless - self-awareness, authenticity, and emotional liberation.

Our exploration will encompass a myriad of topics, including:

Understanding the Nature of Shadows: Shedding light on the unconscious, and spiritual, exploring its origins and significance in shaping our lives.

Confronting the Inner Demons: Courageously acknowledging our suppressed emotions, fears, and traumas, inviting them into the healing embrace of acceptance.

Embracing the Sacred Wounds: Recognizing that our deepest wounds hold the potential for profound growth and empowerment.

Transcending Dualities: Embracing the interplay of light and darkness within us, finding harmony and balance that lead us to a better and complete version of who we are. Cultivating Self-Compassion: Learning to be gentle with ourselves as we navigate the complexities of our inner world, the mind, the spirit and the soul.

Integrating the Shadow Self: Embracing our wholeness by integrating our shadow aspects into the tapestry of the spirit of who we are in the moment of our existence.

As we embark on this voyage of self and spiritual-discovery, remember that Shadow Work is not about striving for perfection but rather about honoring our imperfections and finding beauty in the raw authenticity of our being. By embracing our shadows, we reclaim the power that resides within us and embark on a profound journey of personal growth and spiritual evolution.

So, let us take the first step together into the depths of our inner landscapes, unafraid and with hearts open, for therein lies the key to unlocking the full potential of our humanity. Welcome to the transformative world of Shadow Work.

Chapter 1: Understanding the Nature of Shadows: The Unconscious

Deep within the labyrinth of the human psyche, the unconscious reigns supreme, shaping our thoughts, emotions, and behaviors without our conscious awareness. It is here, in the realm of shadows, that our deepest desires, fears, and unresolved experiences reside. In this chapter, we will embark on a journey to unravel the enigma of the unconscious, shedding light on its origins, significance, and its profound impact on our spiritual lives.

The relationship between the human psyche and the spirit is a complex and profound one, intertwining the realms of psychology and spirituality. The human psyche refers to the totality of an individual's mind, including thoughts, emotions, beliefs, memories, and unconscious processes. On the other hand, the spirit encompasses the essence of a person's being, often associated with their deepest sense of self, higher consciousness, and connection to something greater than themselves.

Perception and Interpretation: The human psyche influences how we perceive and interpret the world around us. Our thoughts, beliefs, and emotional states shape our experiences and interactions, which, in turn, affect our spiritual understanding. Positive or negative mental patterns can influence our spiritual outlook and perception of meaning and purpose in life.

Emotional State and Spiritual Connection: Our emotional well-being significantly impacts our spiritual connection, what we believe in and our sense of purpose. When we experience inner peace, joy, and contentment, it is easier to connect with our spiritual nature and feel a sense of oneness with the universe or higher power no matter our beliefs. Conversely, when we are burdened with emotional turmoil or negativity, our spiritual connection may be hindered, leading to feelings of disconnection and disbelief, not only in ourselves but in our place in the universe.

Shadow Work and Spiritual Growth: Addressing the unconscious aspects of the human psyche through shadow work can profoundly impact spiritual growth. By acknowledging and integrating suppressed emotions, traumas, and unresolved issues, we gain a deeper understanding of ourselves and enhance our spiritual journey. Embracing our shadows can lead to greater compassion, self-awareness, and a more authentic connection with our spiritual essence.

Beliefs and Spiritual Framework: The beliefs held within the psyche play a significant role in shaping one's spiritual framework. Cultural, religious, or philosophical beliefs can influence how individuals perceive the nature of the divine, the afterlife, and the purpose of existence. Exploring and questioning these beliefs can lead to spiritual evolution and a broader understanding of spirituality.

Meditation and Mindfulness: Practices like meditation and mindfulness can positively impact both the psyche and the spirit. These practices help quiet the mind, reduce stress, and increase self-awareness. Through meditation, individuals may experience moments of spiritual insight, transcendence, or a deepening connection to their spiritual essence.

Transcending Ego: The human psyche is closely intertwined with the ego, which often seeks validation, security, and self-preservation. However, the ego can also create barriers to spiritual growth by reinforcing a sense of separation and self-centeredness. Overcoming egoic tendencies and cultivating humility and selflessness can lead to a deeper spiritual understanding and a sense of interconnectedness with all of existence.

Intuition and Inner Guidance: The human psyche is not solely bound to rational thinking; it also encompasses intuition and inner guidance. Honoring and trusting these inner aspects can lead to spiritual insights, as intuition often serves as a channel through which spiritual wisdom and higher truths are conveyed.

Ultimately, the human psyche and the spirit are intricately connected aspects of our being. How we perceive and engage with our psyche can profoundly impact our spiritual journey and vice versa. By cultivating self-awareness, embracing our shadows, and exploring the depths of our consciousness, we pave the way for a more profound and transformative spiritual experience. Integrating psychological understanding with spiritual exploration allows for a holistic approach to personal growth and self-realization.

Exploring the Depths: The Unconscious Mind

The unconscious mind, as proposed by Sigmund Freud and later expanded upon by Carl Jung, represents the vast reservoir of thoughts, memories, and experiences that lie beyond the conscious realm. It is the storehouse of our forgotten dreams, repressed traumas, and unacknowledged emotions. Understanding the workings of the unconscious is essential for embarking on the path of Shadow Work.

What can we do to explore our unconscious mind?

Exploring the depths of the subconscious mind can be a transformative and enlightening journey, offering valuable insights into our thoughts, emotions, behaviors and spirit. Here are some practices and techniques to help you delve into your subconscious:

Meditation: Regular meditation allows you to quiet the conscious mind and access deeper layers of awareness. Focus on your breath or use guided meditation that encourages self-exploration and visualization. As you become more skilled in meditation, you may access memories, emotions, and intuitive insights hidden within the subconscious.

Journaling: Keep a journal to record your thoughts, dreams, and emotions. Writing can help you process subconscious content and make connections between seemingly unrelated aspects of your life. Free-writing or stream-of-consciousness journaling can be especially useful to bypass the censoring mind and access deeper layers of consciousness.

Dream Analysis: Pay attention to your dreams and keep a dream journal. Dreams can provide valuable insights into the subconscious mind's symbols, patterns, and unresolved issues. Analyzing your dreams regularly can help you understand hidden emotions and desires.

Creative Expression: Engage in creative activities like art, music, dance, or writing. These forms of expression can help bypass the conscious mind's filters, allowing subconscious material to surface. Engaging in creative endeavors can lead to powerful insights and emotional release.

Self-Reflection: Set aside time for introspection and self-reflection. Ask yourself deep and meaningful questions about your life, beliefs, and emotions. Explore your past experiences and how they may influence your present behavior and thought patterns.

Mindfulness: Practice mindfulness to become more present in your daily life. By being fully aware of your thoughts and emotions as they arise, you can identify recurring patterns and gain insight into your subconscious motivations.

Regression Therapy: Consider working with a trained therapist experienced in regression therapy. This approach allows you to revisit past memories, experiences, and emotions that may be influencing your current thoughts and behaviors.

Hypnosis: Hypnotherapy can be a helpful tool to access the subconscious mind and explore memories and emotions that may be otherwise hidden from conscious awareness.

Shadow Work: As mentioned in the previous, shadow work involves acknowledging and integrating suppressed or denied aspects of yourself. Engaging in shadow work allows you to explore the deeper layers of your psyche and heal unresolved wounds.

Personal Development Workshops and Retreats: Participate in workshops or retreats focused on self-discovery and personal growth. These settings provide a supportive environment for exploring your subconscious with the guidance of experienced facilitators.

Remember, exploring the subconscious mind can bring up intense emotions and memories. Be gentle with yourself and practice self-compassion throughout this journey. If you encounter significant emotional challenges, consider seeking support from a qualified mental health professional to help you navigate and process your experiences.

Archetypes: The Ancient Blueprints

Jung introduced the concept of archetypes, universal patterns of human experience that reside within the collective unconscious. These primordial forces shape our behavior, influencing our perceptions, choices, and relationships. Exploring the archetypes within ourselves allows us to uncover hidden aspects of our identities and connect with the larger tapestry of humanity.

Ancient archetypes, deeply rooted in the collective unconscious, play a profound role in spiritual growth and self-realization. These primordial patterns, as proposed by Carl Jung, are universal symbols and themes that are found across cultures, religions, and mythologies. They represent core aspects of the human experience and hold valuable wisdom for those on a spiritual journey. Here's how ancient archetypes relate to spiritual growth:

Self-Discovery and Integration: Archetypes act as mirrors, reflecting different facets of our inner world. By recognizing and understanding the archetypal energies within us, we gain insight into our motivations, desires, and fears. This self-discovery enables us to integrate both our light and shadow aspects, fostering a more balanced and harmonious spiritual path.

Transcendence of Ego: Archetypes can provide a framework for understanding the ego's role in our lives. As we explore archetypal patterns, we become more aware of egoic tendencies and can work towards transcending the limitations they impose. This process of ego-transcendence is crucial for achieving higher levels of consciousness and spiritual growth.

Connection to the Collective Unconscious: Ancient archetypes are not limited to individual experiences; they connect us to the collective unconscious, a vast reservoir of shared human experiences and wisdom. Through this connection, spiritual seekers tap into a broader understanding of humanity and find a sense of interconnectedness with all living beings.Symbolic Guidance: Archetypes offer symbolic guidance on the spiritual journey. For example, the "Hero's Journey" archetype often seen in myths and stories reflects the transformative process of self-discovery and spiritual growth. Understanding these archetypal narratives can provide inspiration and guidance during challenging times, encouraging us to persevere and evolve.

Cultural and Religious Significance: Ancient archetypes frequently feature in religious and spiritual traditions. By exploring these archetypal motifs present in various belief systems, we gain a broader perspective on spirituality and its common themes. This broader understanding can enrich our own spiritual practice and foster respect for diverse paths to enlightenment.

Embodying Divine Qualities: Many archetypes represent divine qualities or universal virtues. By embodying these archetypal attributes, such as courage, compassion, wisdom, or love, we align ourselves with higher principles and elevate our spiritual consciousness.

Awakening the Soul's Purpose: Archetypes can help us uncover and embrace our soul's purpose. As we identify with certain archetypal energies, we recognize our unique gifts and calling in life. Embracing our soul's purpose fosters a deep sense of fulfillment and direction on the spiritual path.

Healing and Transformation: Working with archetypes can facilitate profound healing and transformation. The symbolic nature of archetypes allows us to approach our wounds and traumas indirectly, making the healing process more accessible and gentler. As we heal and transform, we become more receptive to spiritual growth.

Incorporating archetypal exploration into spiritual practices can bring depth and richness to the journey of self-discovery. Whether through meditation, dream analysis, or creative expression, engaging with ancient archetypes empowers us to embrace our innate potential and align with the greater mysteries of life. By delving into the realm of archetypes, we embark on a transformative quest towards spiritual growth, understanding, and self-realization.

Chapter 2: The Shadow Self: Embracing the Dark Mirror the Dreams of the Shadow

At the heart of the unconscious lies the Shadow Self, a term coined by Jung. The Shadow embodies the aspects of ourselves that we repress, deny, or deem unacceptable. It encompasses our hidden fears, insecurities, and unresolved conflicts. Engaging with the Shadow Self is a crucial step in Shadow Work, as it unveils our hidden potential and paves the way for profound self-transformation.

Applying the concept of embracing the dark mirror to spiritual work can be a transformative and enlightening process. Here's how you can incorporate this approach into your spiritual journey:

Self-Reflection and Awareness: Engage in regular self-reflection and cultivate self-awareness. Explore your thoughts, emotions, and behaviors with a non-judgmental attitude. Recognize moments when you react strongly to situations or people, as these reactions can often be a mirror reflecting aspects of your shadow self.

Shadow Work Practices: Integrate specific shadow work practices into your spiritual routine. This may involve journaling about your shadow aspects, practicing guided meditations to meet and embrace your shadow self, or engaging in creative expression to explore hidden emotions and experiences.

Dream Analysis: Pay attention to your dreams and analyze them for symbolic representations of your shadow self. Dreams can offer valuable insights into your unconscious mind and provide opportunities to confront and integrate shadow aspects.

Compassion and Forgiveness: Embrace compassion and forgiveness towards yourself and your shadow self. Instead of condemning or berating yourself for your perceived flaws, practice self-compassion and recognize that everyone has a shadow. Treat yourself with the same kindness and understanding you would offer to a dear friend.

Symbolic Language: Dreams speak to us in a symbolic language, bypassing the rational mind and connecting directly with the unconscious. These symbols carry deep meanings and archetypal patterns that are rooted in the collective unconscious. By interpreting dream symbols, we gain access to the hidden realms of our psyche and the spiritual aspects of our being. Dream interpretation is a good practice that can be incorporated when doing shadow work. The shadow will always find a way to speak to you and dreams are one of them.

Access to the Unconscious: During sleep, the conscious mind takes a backseat, allowing the unconscious to come to the forefront. Dreams can act as a doorway to our deepest fears, desires, and unresolved emotions, offering glimpses of the spirit's realm that may be hidden during waking hours.

Guidance and Wisdom: Dreams can provide guidance and wisdom from the higher self or spiritual realms. They may offer insights into life's challenges, choices, and spiritual growth. Paying attention to recurring dreams or vivid dream experiences can lead to transformative realizations and personal revelations.

Communication with the Divine: In some spiritual traditions, dreams are seen as a means of communication with the divine or higher powers. It is believed that the spirit realm can send messages or guidance through dreams, offering spiritual teachings and inspiration.

Healing and Integration: Dreams can aid in the healing process by bringing repressed emotions, memories, and traumas to the surface. Engaging with these dream experiences allows us to integrate these aspects and promote emotional healing and spiritual growth.

Exploration of Past Lives: Some spiritual practitioners and believers in reincarnation use dreams as a tool to explore past lives. These dreams can offer insights into karmic patterns, soul lessons, and connections to previous incarnations.

Is it possible to engage in shadow work while dreaming?

Yes, it is possible to engage in shadow work while dreaming. Dreaming provides a unique opportunity to access and explore the unconscious aspects of ourselves, including the shadow. Shadow work in dreams involves actively engaging with and integrating the shadow aspects that arise during the dream state. Here are some techniques you can use to facilitate shadow work while dreaming:

Lucid Dreaming: Lucid dreaming is when you become aware that you are dreaming while in the dream itself. Once you achieve lucidity, you can actively engage with the dream and consciously explore the shadow elements that arise. This can involve confronting fears, facing challenging situations, or consciously interacting with dream characters that represent aspects of your shadow.

Dream Incubation: Before going to sleep, set an intention or ask a specific question related to your shadow work. This can help direct your dreams towards exploring those aspects. By focusing your attention on the shadow during the dream incubation process, you increase the likelihood of encountering relevant shadow material in your dreams.

Active Imagination: Active imagination is a technique developed by Carl Jung, which involves entering a dialogue with the contents of your unconscious mind. Before going to sleep, visualize or imagine yourself entering a dream space where you can encounter and communicate with the aspects of your shadow. Engage in conversations, ask questions, and explore the underlying emotions or conflicts related to the shadow elements that emerge.

Dream Integration: After you wake up from a dream, take the time to reflect on and journal about the dream. Analyze the symbols, emotions, and events that occurred. Look for connections to your waking life, past experiences, or unresolved issues. This reflective practice can help you gain insight into your shadow and provide opportunities for further exploration and integration.

Dream integration for spiritual shadow work involves using the experiences and insights gained from your dreams to deepen your understanding of the self and promote personal growth on a spiritual level. In the context of shadow work, dream integration can be a powerful tool to explore and confront the hidden, unconscious aspects of yourself and bring them into conscious awareness for healing and transformation.

Here are the key steps involved in dream integration for spiritual shadow work:

Dream Recall: Cultivate the habit of remembering your dreams by keeping a dream journal or recording your dreams immediately upon waking. This practice helps you capture the details of your dreams, including symbols, emotions, and any recurring themes or characters that may have significance.

Dream Analysis: Take time to reflect on your dreams and analyze their potential meanings. Look for patterns, symbols, and emotions that may point to aspects of your shadow self. Dreams often use metaphors and symbols to represent deeper psychological truths, and by analyzing them, you can gain insights into your unconscious mind.

Shadow Exploration: Pay special attention to dreams that evoke strong emotions, fears, or discomfort. These dreams often hold clues to unresolved issues or suppressed aspects of yourself that need attention. Engage in self-inquiry to explore why certain dream scenarios trigger such responses and what they might reveal about your shadow self.

Journaling and Reflection: Write down your dream interpretations and any insights you gain during the dream analysis process. Journaling can help you process your thoughts and emotions, facilitating a deeper understanding of the messages your dreams convey.

Active Imagination: As mentioned before, active imagination is a technique developed by Carl Jung that involves entering a dialogue with the contents of your unconscious. During dream integration, you can use active imagination to further explore and interact with dream symbols, dream characters, and aspects of your shadow that appeared in your dreams.

Intention Setting: Before going to sleep, set an intention to continue your shadow work in your dreams. You can ask for guidance, clarity, or specific experiences related to your spiritual growth and shadow integration.

Meditation: Incorporate meditation or mindfulness practices into your daily routine to enhance your awareness of your emotions, thoughts, and behaviors. This increased self-awareness can also extend into your dream experiences.

Compassion and Self-Acceptance: Throughout the dream integration process, remember to approach yourself with compassion and self-acceptance. Shadow work can be challenging and may bring up uncomfortable emotions, but it's crucial to treat yourself with kindness as you explore and integrate these aspects of yourself.

Dream integration for spiritual shadow work is an ongoing and deeply personal process. It requires patience, commitment, and a willingness to delve into the depths of your psyche. Integrating the insights gained from your dreams into your waking life can lead to profound spiritual growth, emotional healing, and a greater sense of wholeness. If needed, consider working with a therapist or spiritual guide to support you on your journey of dream exploration and shadow integration.

Transcendence and expanded consciousness can play important roles in spiritual shadow work, as they offer pathways to explore and integrate the deeper aspects of the self. Here's how these concepts relate to spiritual shadow work:

Transcendence: Transcendence refers to going beyond ordinary or limited states of consciousness. In the context of shadow work, transcendence involves moving beyond the ego's defenses and conditioned patterns to access higher levels of awareness and understanding. This can allow you to perceive your shadow aspects more objectively and with less judgment.

Transcendence can be achieved through various practices, such as meditation, mindfulness, breathwork, and contemplative practices. By quieting the mind and expanding your awareness, you can become more attuned to the underlying emotions, beliefs, and unresolved issues that constitute your shadow self.

Transcendence also helps you detach from the identification with the ego, which can be particularly beneficial during shadow work. As you identify with your ego's defenses, you become more open to accepting and integrating the aspects of yourself that were previously denied or rejected.

Expanded Consciousness: Expanded consciousness involves broadening your awareness beyond the confines of the individual self to connect with the interconnectedness of all things. This heightened awareness can provide a more holistic perspective on your shadow self, recognizing that these aspects are part of the human experience shared by all.

Practices that induce altered states of consciousness, such as shamanic journeying, psychedelics (where legal and safe), or deep spiritual experiences, can lead to expanded consciousness. In these states, you may gain insights into the collective unconscious and encounter archetypal symbols and energies that are relevant to your shadow work.

Expanded consciousness can facilitate a deeper understanding of the universal themes present in the shadow, helping you to recognize that you are not alone in facing these challenges. This recognition can foster compassion and empathy toward yourself and others as you navigate the complexities of shadow work.

Combining transcendence and expanded consciousness with spiritual shadow work can be a powerful and transformative journey. However, it's essential to approach these practices with respect, discernment, and safety. Engaging in shadow work while transcending the limitations of the ego and exploring expanded states of consciousness requires a grounded and responsible approach.

Always remember that the ultimate goal of spiritual shadow work is not to eliminate the shadow but to integrate it, leading to greater self-awareness, healing, and personal growth. If you find that these practices become overwhelming or unmanageable, seek guidance from experienced practitioners or spiritual mentors to help you navigate the process effectively and safely.

Connection to the Collective Unconscious: Dreams are not only personal experiences but can also connect us to the collective unconscious, where shared symbols and archetypes reside. This connection allows us to access the collective wisdom of humanity and understand the universal aspects of the human spirit.

To harness the power of dreams as a portal to the unconscious spirit, it is essential to practice dream recall, keeping a dream journal, and engaging in dream analysis and interpretation. By nurturing a conscious relationship with our dreams, we can unlock the spiritual and transformative potential they offer, enriching our spiritual journey and deepening our understanding of the self and the cosmos.

Connecting to the collective unconscious for spiritual shadow work involves accessing the deeper layers of the psyche where universal symbols, archetypes, and shared human experiences reside. The collective unconscious, a concept introduced by Carl Jung, is a reservoir of inherited experiences and knowledge common to all of humanity. Here are some methods to help you connect with the collective unconscious for spiritual shadow work:

Shadow Integration in Rituals: Incorporate shadow integration practices into your spiritual rituals and ceremonies. Create sacred space and invite the shadow self to reveal itself. Embrace and acknowledge these aspects, and then consciously integrate them into your whole being.

What are shadow integration rituals?

Shadow integration rituals are ceremonial practices designed to facilitate the process of acknowledging, embracing, and integrating the aspects of your shadow self into your conscious awareness. These rituals can be deeply transformative and can help you bring the hidden or repressed parts of yourself to light, fostering self-acceptance and personal growth. The specific elements and structure of shadow integration rituals may vary based on individual preferences, cultural backgrounds, and spiritual beliefs. Here are some common components you might find in such rituals:

Setting Sacred Space: Begin by creating a sacred space for your ritual. This can involve cleansing the space with sage or incense, setting up an altar with symbolic objects, and inviting spiritual guides or allies to support you during the process.

Self-Reflection: Take time to reflect on the aspects of your shadow that you wish to integrate. Journal about your feelings, fears, past experiences, and any patterns that you recognize in your behavior. Clarify your intentions for the ritual and what you hope to achieve through shadow integration.

Visualization and Meditation: Engage in visualization or meditation practices to connect with your inner self. Journey into your subconscious mind, and imagine meeting the different aspects of your shadow. Embrace these aspects with compassion and acceptance, acknowledging that they are a part of your human experience.

The shadow within holds the truth we fear to see,

Yet in its depths, our greatest strength can be.

Embrace the dark, for it mirrors the light,

In knowing both, we rise to greater height.

Chapter 3 Confronting Shadows: Ceremonial and Ritualistic practices

Working with Deities and Spirits

In some rituals, participants may symbolically confront their shadows through various means, such as role-playing or using props. This process helps externalize the aspects of the shadow, making them more tangible and easier to work with during the integration.Writing a Letter: Write a letter to your shadow, expressing your willingness to acknowledge and integrate it. Share your commitment to growth and self-understanding, assuring your shadow that you are ready to face and accept its presence in your life.

When it comes to a more ceremonial practice, we can always include the spirits and deities we work with. Shadow work can be done with deities or gods/goddesses from various spiritual or religious traditions. Working with deities in shadow work can provide additional support, guidance, and symbolism as you explore and integrate your shadow aspects. Here's how you can incorporate deities into your shadow work practice:

Deity Selection: Choose a deity or deities that resonate with the aspects of your shadow you wish to work with. Different deities represent various archetypal energies and can be associated with specific themes or aspects of the human experience. For example, Kali in Hinduism represents transformation and the destruction of egoic patterns, while Hades in Greek mythology embodies the realm of the underworld and the hidden depths of the psyche.

Invocation and Prayer: Begin your shadow work session by invoking the presence of the deity or deities you have chosen to work with. Offer prayers or invocations, expressing your intention to explore and integrate your shadow aspects with their assistance and guidance. Seek their blessings and support in your journey of self-discovery and transformation.

Symbolic Associations: Explore the symbolism associated with the chosen deity and how it relates to your shadow work. Deities and stories connected to the deity can provide insights and reflections on the aspects of your shadow you are working with. Incorporate these symbols into your rituals or meditations as visualizations or altar decorations to strengthen the connection and deepen the exploration.

Archetypal Reflection: Consider the qualities and characteristics of the deity you are working with as archetypal representations of the energies you are exploring in your shadow. Reflect on how these qualities manifest within you and how they can guide your understanding and integration of your shadow aspects.

Offerings and Devotion: Offerings and acts of devotion can deepen your connection with the deity and create a sacred space for shadow work. This can include lighting candles, burning incense, offering food or drink, or performing rituals specific to the deity's tradition. These offerings symbolize your dedication and reverence to the process of shadow work with the deity's assistance.

Meditation and Visualization: Engage in meditation and visualization practices to connect with the energy and wisdom of the deity. Visualize the deity guiding you through your shadow work, offering insights, and supporting your integration process. You can imagine having conversations with the deity or receiving teachings and messages that help you better understand and work with your shadow aspects.

Rituals and Ceremonies: Design rituals or ceremonies specifically tailored to your deity and the aspects of your shadow you are exploring. These rituals can include symbolic actions, prayers, chants, or other practices that invoke the presence of the deity and create a sacred space for deep introspection and healing.

When working with deities in shadow work, it is important to approach them with respect, humility, and an open heart. Be mindful of cultural and religious contexts and ensure that your work is done in a way that aligns with your personal beliefs and practices. Additionally, if you are not familiar with a specific deity or tradition, it can be helpful to study and understand their symbolism, mythology, and cultural significance to ensure a respectful and meaningful engagement.

When it comes to deities are archetypal symbols, and their energy and significance can be interpreted in various ways depending on the individual's personal beliefs and experiences.

This doesn't mean only that the deity will guide you but also what they represent as a devotee or follower will do for you.

There are numerous deities from various mythologies and spiritual traditions that can be a good match for spiritual shadow work. The choice of deity may depend on your personal connection, cultural background, or the specific aspects of your shadow you wish to explore. Here are a few deities known for their associations with transformation, the underworld, and shadow-related themes:

Kali (Hinduism): Kali is a powerful goddess in Hindu mythology associated with destruction, transformation, and the fierce aspects of femininity. She represents the process of annihilating the ego and transcending limitations, making her an ideal guide for shadow work and inner transformation.

Hades/Pluto (Greek/Roman Mythology): Hades is the god of the underworld in Greek mythology, and his Roman counterpart is Pluto. He rules over the realm of the dead and the hidden depths of the psyche. Working with Hades or Pluto can assist in exploring the darker aspects of the self and the subconscious mind.

Persephone (Greek Mythology): Persephone is the Queen of the Underworld and the daughter of Demeter, the goddess of agriculture and fertility. She embodies themes of transformation, rebirth, and the journey between the realms of light and darkness.

Working with Persephone can help navigate the process of descending into the shadow and embracing its gifts.

Inanna/Ishtar (Sumerian/Babylonian Mythology): Inanna, also known as Ishtar, is a goddess of love, war, and fertility. She undertakes a descent into the underworld, facing trials and sacrifices, as a symbol of death and rebirth. Working with Inanna can provide insights into the cyclical nature of the psyche and the transformational power of shadow work.

Osiris (Egyptian Mythology): Osiris is an ancient Egyptian god of death, resurrection, and fertility. His myth involves dismemberment and resurrection, symbolizing the cyclical nature of life and death. Working with Osiris can help in exploring themes of transformation and the journey through the darkness to find renewal and growth.

Cerridwen (Celtic Mythology): Cerridwen is a Celtic goddess associated with wisdom, magic, and transformation. She possesses a cauldron of inspiration, wherein the transformative brew simmers. Working with Cerridwen can aid in exploring the transformative powers of the subconscious and the wisdom found in the shadow.

Ereshkigal (Sumerian Mythology): Ereshkigal is the Sumerian goddess of the underworld, associated with death, rebirth, and shadow aspects. Working with Ereshkigal can assist in understanding the depths of the psyche and the importance of embracing the shadow for personal growth.

Amaterasu (Japanese Mythology): Amaterasu is the Shinto goddess of the sun and light, but her myth also includes a period of self-isolation in a cave, which symbolizes a descent into the darkness of the shadow. Working with Amaterasu can help explore themes of balance between light and dark within oneself.

Pele (Hawaiian Mythology): Pele is the Hawaiian goddess of fire, volcanoes, and transformation. Working with Pele can aid in exploring the fiery aspects of the shadow, bringing forth deep-seated emotions and passions for healing and integration.

Mama Brigitte (Vodou): In Haitian Vodou, Maman Brigitte is a powerful lwa associated with death, the underworld, and the cemetery. She can be called upon for guidance and protection during shadow work related to ancestral healing and understanding the mysteries of life and death.

The Morrigan (Celtic Mythology): The Morrigan is a Celtic goddess associated with war, fate, and transformation. She embodies both the light and dark aspects of the feminine and can help navigate the complexities of shadow work.

Sedna (Inuit Mythology): Sedna is an Inuit goddess of the sea and marine creatures. Her myth involves being cast into the sea and residing in the depths, representing the subconscious mind. Working with Sedna can aid in exploring the depths of the unconscious and the hidden aspects of the self.

Xolotl (Aztec Mythology): Xolotl is an Aztec god associated with death, transformation, and the underworld. He guides souls to the afterlife and can assist in shadow work involving the journey through darkness and embracing the transformative power of change.

Nyx (Greek Mythology): Nyx is the primordial goddess of the night and darkness. Working with Nyx can aid in embracing the mysteries of the shadow and finding solace in the depths of the psyche.

These are some examples of some deities that can be incorporated into the shadow work practices. Now I will give you a personal experience when working with deities when doing shadow work. As a practitioner, spiritualist and a witch I work very closely with the Goddess Hekate, she has been an important part of my shadow work.

WORKING WITH HEKATE:

Working with **Hekate** can be a powerful and transformative approach to spiritual shadow work. Hekate is an ancient goddess with roots in Greek, Roman, and various other mythological traditions. She is often associated with liminality, crossroads, magic, and the realms of life, death, and the underworld. Here are some ways in which Hekate can assist you in your spiritual shadow work:

Psychopomp Guide: As a goddess with connections to the underworld and the journey between worlds, Hekate can serve as a psychopomp, guiding you through the depths of your psyche during your shadow work. She can help you navigate the inner realms, uncovering hidden aspects of yourself and facilitating your exploration of the shadow.

Embracing the Crossroads: Hekate is often depicted at crossroads, which symbolize points of choice and transformation. Engaging with Hekate in your shadow work can help you embrace the crossroads of your own life, face difficult decisions, and understand the multiplicity of choices within your psyche.

Magic and Transformation: Hekate is known as a goddess of magic and transformation. Invoking her during your shadow work can amplify the potency of your inner work, supporting you in transforming negative patterns, releasing old wounds, and integrating your shadow aspects.

Protection and Strength: Hekate is also associated with protection and strength. When engaging in deep shadow work, it's essential to feel supported and safe. Call upon Hekate to provide guidance and courage as you delve into the depths of your psyche.

Honoring the Dark and Light: Hekate embodies the duality of light and dark, making her a fitting guide for shadow work. She can help you come to terms with the various aspects of your shadow and recognize that both light and dark elements are integral parts of your wholeness.

Rituals and Offerings: Create rituals and offerings to Hekate as a way of inviting her assistance and guidance in your shadow work. Offerings may include candles, incense, herbs, or symbolic items that represent your intentions for the work you wish to undertake.

Inner Wisdom and Intuition: Hekate is associated with wisdom and intuition, and she can help you access your inner knowledge during your shadow work. Trust your intuition and the guidance you may receive from Hekate as you explore the depths of your psyche.

To give you a more clear example with Hekate let talk a little about Hekate Brimo. Yes, Hekate Brimo can be a powerful aspect of Hekate to work with for spiritual shadow work. Hekate

Brimo, often referred to as the "Angry One" or "Terrifying One," represents a fierce and potent aspect of the goddess. While her name might evoke feelings of fear or intimidation, it is essential to understand that this aspect of Hekate is not inherently negative but rather embodies the intensity and power required for profound transformation and shadow work.

When working with Hekate Brimo for spiritual shadow work:

Embrace the Intensity: Hekate Brimo's intensity can mirror the depth and intensity of the shadow aspects you are exploring. Embrace the power within yourself to confront the hidden and challenging parts of your psyche, recognizing that this process may require courage and strength.

Confronting Fears: Hekate Brimo can assist you in confronting your fears and deeply ingrained patterns. Her fierce presence can help you face the aspects of your shadow that you might have avoided or suppressed.

Embodying Inner Strength: By connecting with Hekate Brimo, you can tap into your inner strength and resilience. This aspect of Hekate can inspire you to move through the transformative journey of shadow work with determination and confidence.

Transformative Fire: Hekate Brimo's energy can be likened to a transformative fire that burns away what no longer serves you. Allow this intensity to assist you in releasing old patterns and beliefs, creating space for personal growth and healing.

Protection and Guidance: As you engage in deep shadow work, call upon Hekate Brimo for protection and guidance. Trust in her fierce wisdom to support you as you navigate the inner realms of your psyche.

Surrender and Release: Working with Hekate Brimo may require an element of surrendering to the process of shadow work. Allow yourself to release the resistance and defenses that may arise during the exploration of your shadow.

Hekate Trivia can also be a valuable aspect of Hekate to work with for spiritual shadow work. Trivia is one of Hekate's epithets, and it is derived from the Latin "trivium," which means "three roads" or "three ways." This aspect of Hekate is associated with crossroads, choices, and the liminal spaces between worlds.

Working with Hekate Trivia for spiritual shadow work can offer the following benefits:

Navigating Choices: Hekate Trivia's association with crossroads symbolizes the points of choice and decision-making in life. In shadow work, exploring the choices that have led to your current patterns and behaviors can help you gain insights into your unconscious motivations and embrace your personal agency in creating positive change.

Embracing Liminality: The liminal spaces where Hekate Trivia presides represent the thresholds between different states of being. Engaging with this aspect can help you embrace the "in-between" moments and acknowledge the transformative potential found in the liminality of your shadow self.

Integrating Duality: Hekate Trivia embodies the concept of duality and the interconnectedness of opposites. Through shadow work, you explore both the light and dark aspects of your psyche, acknowledging that both are essential parts of your wholeness.

Inner Alchemy: Hekate Trivia's presence at the crossroads can symbolize the process of inner alchemy, where you transmute and integrate your shadow aspects into a higher state of self-awareness and personal growth.

Illuminating Choices and Patterns: Working with Hekate Trivia can help shed light on the choices and patterns that have shaped your life and led to your shadow aspects. This awareness can be transformative and empowering as you take responsibility for your growth and healing.

Seeking Guidance: At crossroads, travelers often seek guidance to choose the right path. Similarly, connecting with Hekate Trivia can provide you with insights, inspiration, and guidance during your shadow work journey.

To incorporate Hekate Trivia into your spiritual shadow work:

Create Sacred Space: Set up a sacred space for your practice, using candles, incense, or other symbolic items to create a sense of reverence and connection.

Invocations and Prayers: Invoke Hekate Trivia through prayers or invocations, expressing your intentions for your shadow work journey.

Meditation and Reflection: Practice meditation or reflective exercises to explore the choices, patterns, and crossroads in your life. Allow Hekate Trivia's energy to illuminate the insights you seek.

Symbolic Rituals: Design rituals or symbolic actions that represent your willingness to explore your shadow aspects and embrace the transformative potential of your journey.

Journaling: Keep a journal to document your experiences, thoughts, and revelations during your shadow work with Hekate Trivia.

Hekate Cthonia can be an excellent aspect of Hekate to work with for spiritual shadow work. The term "Cthonia" is derived from the Greek word "chthonios," which means "of the earth" or "underworld." As such, Hekate Cthonia is associated with the depths of the earth and the hidden realms, making her a potent guide for exploring and integrating your shadow aspects.

Working with Hekate Cthonia for spiritual shadow work can offer the following benefits:

Embracing the Underworld: Hekate Cthonia's connection to the underworld represents the depths of the psyche and the hidden aspects of the self. She can assist you in delving into the subconscious, bringing to light repressed emotions, fears, and unresolved issues.

Inner Transformation: As a goddess of the underworld, Hekate Cthonia is associated with transformation and renewal. She can support you in the process of releasing old patterns, healing wounds, and embracing personal growth.

Confronting the Shadow: Hekate Cthonia's presence can provide the courage and strength needed to face your shadow aspects and work through any challenges that arise during the process.

Ancestral Connection: In some traditions, Hekate Cthonia is associated with ancestral spirits and the wisdom of the past. Working with her can help you explore ancestral patterns and inherited traits that may be influencing your shadow aspects.

Wisdom and Intuition: Hekate Cthonia is a goddess of wisdom and intuition. She can guide you in tapping into your inner knowing and understanding the symbolic messages within your shadow.

Honoring Darkness and Light: Like other aspects of Hekate, Hekate Cthonia embodies the duality of light and dark. In shadow work, it's essential to acknowledge and integrate both aspects, recognizing that they are integral parts of your wholeness.

To incorporate Hekate Cthonia into your spiritual shadow work:

Set Intentions: Clearly state your intentions for your shadow work journey and your desire to work with Hekate Cthonia as your guide and ally.

Rituals and Offerings: Design rituals or offerings that honor Hekate Cthonia's connection to the underworld. Consider using earth-related elements such as stones, soil, or plants in your rituals.

Meditation and Visualization: Practice meditation or visualization to connect with Hekate Cthonia's energy and explore the depths of your psyche with her guidance.

Dreamwork: Hekate Cthonia is also associated with dreams and the subconscious. Pay attention to your dreams during this time, as they may provide insights into your shadow aspects.

Journaling: Keep a journal to record your experiences, thoughts, and emotions during your shadow work with Hekate Cthonia.

Hekate Phosphoros, also known as "Light-Bringer" or "Torchbearer," can be a beneficial aspect of Hekate to work with for spiritual shadow work. While Hekate is often associated with the darkness and the underworld, her aspect as Phosphoros embodies the transformative power of bringing light into the darkness.

Working with Hekate Phosphoros for spiritual shadow work can offer the following benefits:

Illuminating the Shadow: Hekate Phosphoros brings light and illumination, which can help you gain clarity and understanding as you explore your shadow aspects. Her torch can metaphorically shine light into the depths of your psyche, revealing hidden patterns and unresolved emotions.

Embracing Awareness: Through the light of Hekate Phosphoros, you can develop greater self-awareness and gain insights into the underlying causes of your shadow aspects. This awareness is crucial for the process of integration and transformation.

Balance of Light and Dark: Hekate Phosphoros embodies the balance between light and dark. In shadow work, it is essential to acknowledge and integrate both aspects of yourself. She can assist you in embracing the full spectrum of your being.

Inner Guidance: As the Torchbearer, Hekate Phosphoros can serve as a guide through your shadow work journey. You can call upon her for assistance and wisdom as you navigate the depths of your psyche.

Transformation and Healing: The light of Hekate Phosphoros brings healing energy that can facilitate the transformation of your shadow aspects. It can help you release old patterns, heal emotional wounds, and foster personal growth.

To incorporate Hekate Phosphoros into your spiritual shadow work:

Set Intentions: Clearly state your intentions for your shadow work journey and your desire to work with Hekate Phosphoros as your guide.

Meditation and Visualization: Practice meditation or visualization to connect with Hekate Phosphoros' light and allow it to shine upon the aspects of your shadow that you wish to explore.

Candle Rituals: Use candles to symbolize Hekate Phosphoros' torch and the illumination it brings. Light candles during your shadow work sessions to invoke her presence.

Journaling: Keep a journal to document your experiences, insights, and reflections during your shadow work with Hekate Phosphoros.

Gratitude and Offerings: Show gratitude and reverence to Hekate Phosphoros through offerings or dedications as a way of honoring her presence in your spiritual journey.

Hekate Kuratrophos can be a potent aspect of Hekate to work with for spiritual shadow work. As the goddess of nurturing and the protector of children, Hekate Kuratrophos brings a caring and compassionate energy that can support you as you delve into your shadow aspects.

Working with Hekate Kuratrophos for spiritual shadow work can offer the following benefits:

Compassionate Exploration: Hekate Kuratrophos' nurturing qualities can create a safe and gentle space for exploring your shadow aspects with compassion and understanding.

Inner Healing: Her nurturing energy can aid in the process of healing emotional wounds and traumas that may be related to your shadow aspects.

Embracing Vulnerability: Hekate Kuratrophos encourages you to embrace vulnerability as you face your shadow aspects, fostering a sense of acceptance and self-compassion.

Inner Child Work: As the protector of children, Hekate Kuratrophos can support you in connecting with your inner child and addressing any unresolved issues from your past that may contribute to your shadow.Unconditional Love: Working with Hekate Kuratrophos can help you cultivate self-love and self-acceptance, essential components of shadow work.

To incorporate Hekate Kuratrophos into your spiritual shadow work:

Set Intentions: Clearly state your intentions for your shadow work journey and your desire to work with Hekate Kuratrophos as a nurturing guide.

Meditation and Visualization: Practice meditation or visualization to connect with Hekate Kuratrophos' nurturing energy. Envision her holding space for your healing and exploration.

Inner Child Work: If you feel called, engage in inner child work to address any unresolved issues from your past that may be influencing your shadow aspects. Allow Hekate Kuratrophos to support you in this process.

Journaling: Keep a journal to record your experiences, emotions, and insights during your shadow work with Hekate Kuratrophos.

Offerings and Gratitude: Show gratitude to Hekate Kuratrophos through offerings or dedications as a way of acknowledging her presence in your healing and growth.

As you can see there are many epithets of Hekate that can be incorporated for shadow work, she is not the only deity that can be of help for this form of healing.

Other examples are:

Neptune, the god of the sea in Roman mythology (equivalent to Poseidon in Greek mythology), is often associated with the depths of the ocean, dreams, and the subconscious. While Neptune's symbolism and attributes can be relevant to certain aspects of spiritual exploration, it's important to consider the specific nature of shadow work and whether Neptune's energy aligns with your intentions.

When it comes to spiritual shadow work, there are various factors to consider in selecting a deity or energy to work with:

Archetypal Alignment: Neptune's association with the subconscious and dreams can be relevant to exploring the depths of the psyche. As a water god, Neptune may represent the emotional and intuitive realms that are often involved in shadow work.

Personal Connection: Your personal relationship and connection with Neptune or any deity play a significant role in the effectiveness of your spiritual work. If you resonate with Neptune's energy or feel a strong affinity for water-related symbolism, he may be a suitable guide for your shadow work.

Supportive Attributes: Consider whether Neptune's attributes, such as introspection, intuition, and emotional exploration, align with the goals of your shadow work journey.

Cultural Context: Respect the cultural context and symbolism associated with Neptune. Ensure that you approach the deity with reverence and an understanding of his traditional role and significance.

Inner Exploration: Neptune's association with dreams and the subconscious can be valuable in inner exploration. Working with Neptune may help you access deeper layers of your psyche during meditation, dreamwork, or other spiritual practices.

However, it's essential to note that Neptune is not typically regarded as a deity specifically associated with shadow work. While his attributes may complement certain aspects of the process, other deities or archetypes might be more directly related to the concept of confronting and integrating the shadow self.

Cernunnos can be a powerful and suitable guide for spiritual shadow work. Cernunnos is a Celtic deity often associated with nature, fertility, the wild, and the cycles of life and death. His connection to the natural world and the cycles of transformation make him a relevant archetype for exploring and integrating shadow aspects.

Here's why Cernunnos can be beneficial for spiritual shadow work:

Nature and Instinctual Energy: Cernunnos represents the untamed and instinctual forces of nature. Working with him can help you connect with your primal instincts and explore the raw and authentic aspects of yourself that may be part of your shadow.

Death and Rebirth: As a deity associated with cycles of life and death, Cernunnos can aid you in understanding the transformative nature of shadow work. Like the changing seasons, shadow work involves the process of death and rebirth, shedding old patterns and embracing new growth.

Embracing Wildness: Cernunnos embodies the wild and primal energy within us. Embracing this aspect can empower you to embrace your authentic self and integrate parts of your psyche that may have been suppressed or denied.

Balance and Wholeness: Cernunnos' antlers are often seen as symbols of balance and harmony. Through shadow work, you seek to find balance between light and dark, integrating all aspects of yourself to achieve a sense of wholeness.

Connection to the Unconscious: Cernunnos' deep connection to nature and the cycles of life can facilitate your exploration of the unconscious mind and the hidden aspects of your psyche.

When working with Cernunnos for spiritual shadow work:

Study and Respect: Take time to learn about Cernunnos and his cultural context within Celtic mythology. Approach his energy with respect and cultural sensitivity.

Nature Connection: Spend time in nature to connect with Cernunnos' essence and the wild energies he embodies. Nature can serve as a powerful catalyst for inner exploration during shadow work.

Ritual and Offerings: Design rituals that honor Cernunnos and his role in your shadow work journey. Consider offerings of herbs, plants, or other symbols of nature as a gesture of reverence.

Meditation and Visualization: Practice meditation or visualization to connect with Cernunnos' energy. Imagine yourself in the presence of the stag god as you delve into your inner psyche.

Journaling: Keep a journal to document your experiences, insights, and reflections during your shadow work with Cernunnos.

I know I mentioned her briefly before, but Persephone can be a meaningful and supportive figure for shadow work. In Greek mythology, Persephone is the daughter of Zeus and Demeter, and she becomes the Queen of the Underworld after being abducted by Hades. Her story is intricately tied to themes of transformation, death, rebirth, and the cycles of life.

Here's why Persephone can be beneficial for spiritual shadow work:

Journey to the Underworld: Persephone's story involves descending into the Underworld, a symbolic representation of exploring the depths of the psyche during shadow work. Her experiences in the Underworld reflect the transformative nature of facing and integrating shadow aspects.

Embracing Darkness: As the Queen of the Underworld, Persephone embraces the darkness and governs the realm of the dead. Working with her can help you come to terms with the shadow aspects within yourself and accept the complexity of your psyche.

Inner Integration: Persephone's journey back and forth between the realms of light and darkness reflects the process of integrating light and shadow within us. She can guide you through the process of acknowledging and accepting all aspects of your being.

Symbol of Rebirth: Persephone's annual return from the Underworld represents the cycle of death and rebirth. Engaging with her energy can support you in shedding old patterns, healing wounds, and experiencing personal growth and renewal. Divine Feminine Wisdom: Persephone is often associated with the divine feminine, and her story contains profound wisdom and insights into the transformative power of the feminine aspects of the psyche.

When working with Persephone for spiritual shadow work:

Study and Connection: Take time to learn about Persephone's myth and significance in Greek mythology. Develop a connection with her through meditation, prayer, or simply contemplating her story.

Inner Exploration: Use Persephone's story as a symbolic framework for your own inner exploration. Reflect on the ways her experiences parallel your own journey of self-discovery and transformation.

Rituals and Offerings: Design rituals to honor Persephone and her role in your shadow work journey. Offerings of flowers, pomegranate seeds, or other symbolic items can be a way to show reverence.

Journaling: Keep a journal to record your experiences, dreams, and insights during your shadow work with Persephone.

Trust Your Intuition: Allow yourself to trust your intuition and inner guidance as you work with Persephone. Embrace her as an ally and guide in your journey of self-awareness and integration.

Persephone's symbolism and myth can provide profound insights and support during your spiritual shadow work. As you engage with her energy, remember to approach the process with respect and an open heart, trusting in the transformative power of embracing your shadow aspects for personal growth and healing.

The god Odin (also known as Woden or Wotan) can be a meaningful and fitting figure for spiritual shadow work. Odin is a complex deity associated with wisdom, knowledge, magic, poetry, and the runes. He is also known as the All-Father, the chief god of the Norse pantheon.

Here's why Odin can be beneficial for spiritual shadow work:

Pursuit of Wisdom: Odin is known for his relentless pursuit of wisdom and knowledge, often sacrificing much to gain greater insights. Shadow work requires a willingness to delve deep into the unknown aspects of the self, and Odin's thirst for wisdom can inspire you to explore and confront your shadow.

Shamanic Journeying: Odin is associated with shamanism and journeying between the realms. He is known to have traveled to the realm of the dead, gaining esoteric knowledge. His shamanic nature can aid you in your journey of inner exploration during shadow work.

Symbol of Sacrifice: Odin's sacrifice of himself to gain the knowledge of the runes exemplifies the idea that self-awareness and understanding come at a price. Shadow work often involves facing uncomfortable truths and letting go of old patterns, requiring courage and sacrifice.

Integration of Dualities: Odin embodies duality and paradox, often appearing as a wise and all-knowing figure while also being associated with the battlefield and war. Working with Odin can help you embrace and integrate the various aspects of your psyche, including both light and shadow.

Rune Magic: Odin's association with runes, ancient symbols of power and wisdom, can be incorporated into your shadow work practice. The runes can serve as powerful tools for inner guidance and self-discovery.

When working with Odin for spiritual shadow work:

Study and Connection: Take time to learn about Odin's myths, his role in Norse mythology, and his cultural significance.

Develop a connection with him through research, meditation, or prayer.

Runes and Divination: If you are drawn to rune magic, incorporate the runes into your shadow work practice. Use them for divination or meditation to gain insights into your unconscious mind.

Meditation and Journeying: Practice meditation or shamanic journeying to connect with Odin's energy. Seek his guidance and wisdom as you explore your shadow aspects.

Journaling: Keep a journal to record your experiences, thoughts, and reflections during your shadow work with Odin.

Trust Your Intuition: Allow yourself to trust your intuition and inner guidance as you work with Odin. Embrace him as an ally and mentor in your journey of self-awareness and integration.

Hel, the Norse goddess of the underworld, can be a powerful and suitable guide for spiritual shadow work. In Norse mythology, Hel rules over the realm of the dead, which is also known as Helheim. Her association with the underworld makes her a relevant figure for exploring and integrating shadow aspects.

Here's why Hel can be beneficial for spiritual shadow work:

Embracing the Shadow: As the goddess of the underworld, Hel embodies the darkness and the hidden aspects of the self.

Working with her can help you confront and embrace your shadow aspects with courage and compassion.

Inner Transformation: Hel's realm represents the realm of transformation and change. Engaging with her energy can facilitate the process of releasing old patterns, healing emotional wounds, and experiencing personal growth.

Death and Rebirth: Hel is connected to the cycles of life, death, and rebirth. Just as she welcomes the souls of the deceased into her realm, she can support you in acknowledging the cycles of transformation and renewal within yourself.

Acceptance and Integration: Hel's acceptance of all souls, regardless of their deeds in life, symbolizes her non-judgmental nature. Through shadow work, you can learn to accept and integrate all aspects of yourself, understanding that your shadow is a natural part of your wholeness.

Ancestral Connection: Hel's role as the ruler of the underworld also connects her to ancestral spirits. Working with her can facilitate exploration of ancestral patterns and inherited traits that may be influencing your shadow.

When working with Hel for spiritual shadow work:

Study and Respect: Take time to learn about Hel's myth and significance in Norse mythology. Approach her with respect and cultural sensitivity.

Meditation and Visualization: Practice meditation or visualization to connect with Hel's energy. Envision yourself in the presence of the goddess as you explore your inner psyche.

Rituals and Offerings: Design rituals that honor Hel and her role in your shadow work journey. Offerings of symbolic items such as dark-colored candles or flowers can be a way to show reverence.

Journaling: Keep a journal to record your experiences, insights, and reflections during your shadow work with Hel.

Inner Journeying: Consider engaging in inner journeying or guided visualizations to visit Helheim and seek her guidance and wisdom.

In Hinduism, there are several deities that can be beneficial for spiritual shadow work. Here are some examples:

Kali is a powerful and fierce goddess associated with destruction, transformation, and liberation. She represents the darker aspect of existence and can help you confront and transmute your shadow aspect. Working with Kali can aid in releasing old patterns, attachments, and limiting beliefs, leading to personal transformation and personal growth.

Shiva is often depicted as the god of destruction and creation. His role as destroyer can assist in letting go of what no longer serves you, including shadow aspects that hinder your growth. Shiva's energy can help you embrace impermanence and facilitate the process of transformation and self-realization.

Durga is a warrior goddess who represents strength, courage, and protection. She can support you in facing and overcoming challenges that arise during your shadow work journey. Durga's energy can provide a sense of inner power and resilience as you navigate the depths of your psyche.

Hanuman is a deity known for his devotion, strength, and loyalty. Working with Hanuman can help you develop the courage and determination needed to confront your shadows. Hanuman's unwavering dedication to righteousness and selfless service can inspire you in your journey of self-discovery and integration.

Kalo Ma, an aspect of the goddess Kali, represents the divine mother and nurturing, compassionate energy of the feminine. Her fierce love and transformative power can guide you through the depths of your shadow aspects, offering support and compassion as you face and heal your wounds.

We could make an entire book on how to do shadow work with deities and spirits, as you can see shadow work can be approached from different spiritual journeys. Shadow work when done with the guidance of a deity can be empowering, this doesn't mean that you need a deity to do it.

The archetypes present in the Goetia can potentially be used in spiritual shadow work, but it is essential to approach this integration with careful consideration and understanding of the complexities involved.

The Goetia is a grimoire that lists 72 spirits or entities, often referred to as demons or daimons which can be invoked or evoked for various purposes. Each spirit in the Goetia is associated with unique attributes, symbols, and characteristics, and they are traditionally perceived as external entities with distinct personalities and powers.

When considering the archetypes of Goetia for shadow work, it's important to recognize that these spirits were historically depicted as personifications of specific energies or aspects of the human psyche. From a psychological perspective, they can be viewed as representations of various psychological forces or inner aspects, including suppressed emotions, desires, fears, and aspects of the unconscious.

In this context, one can explore the archetypes of the Goetia in shadow work as a way of tapping into and understanding different facets of their psyche. By personifying these aspects and engaging with them through visualization, meditation, or symbolic rituals, individuals can gain insights into their hidden or repressed aspects and explore the underlying spiritual and psychological themes they represent.

However, working with such archetypes requires a responsible and ethical approach, as well as a deep understanding of psychological symbolism and spiritual practices. Engaging with these archetypes should not be taken lightly, especially by individuals who are inexperienced or lack proper training in psychological or spiritual work.

If you are interested in incorporating archetypes from the Goetia or any other system into your shadow work, consider the following:

Study: Take the time to thoroughly research and study the archetypes of the Goetia and their historical context. Understanding the symbolism and cultural significance is essential to approach these practices with respect and mindfulness.

Intentions: Be clear about your intentions for working with these archetypes. Are you seeking psychological insights, healing, or personal growth? Ensure that your motivations are grounded and aligned with positive, ethical objectives.

Expertise: If you are new to shadow work or working with archetypes, consider seeking guidance from a qualified therapist, counselor, or spiritual mentor with experience in these practices.

They can provide support and help you navigate any challenges that may arise.

Ethics: Approach your shadow work with a strong ethical foundation. Ensure that your practices are done with integrity, respect for yourself and others, and an awareness of the potential impact on your mental and emotional well-being.

Remember that shadow work is a deeply personal and transformative process. While archetypes from various systems, including the Goetia, can be informative and powerful tools for self-discovery, always prioritize your safety, well-being, and ethical considerations in your spiritual journey.

Chapter 4: Confronting Our Inner demons

Courageously acknowledging our suppressed emotions, fears, and traumas, inviting them into the healing embrace of acceptance.

The first thing we need to understand is who our inner demons are. In shadow work, "inner demons" refer to the hidden or suppressed aspects of ourselves that we may not be aware of or may try to avoid. These inner demons are usually composed of repressed emotions, unresolved traumas, negative beliefs, and aspects of our personality that we reject or deny. These elements often reside in our subconscious, influencing our thoughts, behaviors, and interactions without our conscious awareness.

In spiritual shadow work, the concept of inner demons takes on a deeper and more profound meaning. Inner demons are not just limited to psychological or emotional aspects but also encompass spiritual and soul-level aspects that are repressed or unacknowledged. These spiritual inner demons can impede our spiritual growth and prevent us from realizing our true potential and connection with the higher self or the divine.

Let's see some examples and differences of our inner demons from different perspectives, you can create a diverse range of inner demons that your characters confront during their shadow work journey.

The Wounded Child: This inner demon represents the unresolved pain and traumas from the character's past that continue to affect their self-esteem, relationships, and emotional well-being.

The Inner Critic: This demon personifies the character's self-doubt, self-criticism, and negative self-talk, which often holds them back from pursuing their dreams and reaching their full potential.

The Fearful Avoider: This demon embodies the character's avoidance of certain emotions or situations due to fear, preventing them from confronting their challenges and achieving personal growth.

The Rageful Shadow: This inner demon represents the character's repressed anger and resentment, which can lead to destructive behavior and strained relationships if not addressed.

The Perfectionist: This demon manifests as an obsession with perfection and fear of failure, hindering the character's ability to take risks and embrace imperfections.

The Martyr: This inner demon is characterized by the character's tendency to put others' needs before their own, leading to self-sacrifice and a lack of healthy boundaries.

The Envious Shadow: This demon represents the character's feelings of jealousy and comparison to others, preventing them from celebrating their achievements and finding contentment.

The Greedy Self: This inner demon embodies the character's insatiable desire for more material possessions or power, leading to a constant dissatisfaction and disconnection from what truly matters.

The Victim: This demon personifies the character's tendency to see themselves as a victim of circumstances, which can lead to a sense of powerlessness and a lack of accountability.

The Shadow Saboteur: This inner demon undermines the character's efforts for success and happiness, sabotaging their relationships, career, or personal endeavors.

As you can see this is more connected to the aspect of us that relates to our reactions and the way we think subconsciously and dominates the way we see life from the shadow perspective. The shadow perspective is the way we see, feel, interpret, and accept how life moves around us creating a false sense of security. Now let's look at this from a more spiritual perspective.

In spiritual shadow work, the concept of inner demons takes on a deeper and more profound meaning. Inner demons are not just limited to psychological or emotional aspects but also encompass spiritual and soul-level aspects that are repressed or unacknowledged. These spiritual inner demons can impede our spiritual growth and prevent us from realizing our true potential and connection with the higher self or the divine.

Here's how inner demons play a role in our spiritual shadow work:

Ego and False Self: The ego, which is the part of us that identifies with our individuality and separateness, can become an inner demon when it becomes overly dominant. It can create illusions, attachments, and false identities that obscure our true nature as spiritual beings.

Attachment and Clinging: The attachment to material possessions, relationships, or beliefs can create inner demons that keep us stuck in the cycle of suffering. Letting go of these attachments is an essential part of spiritual growth.

Negative Thought Patterns: Spiritual shadow work involves examining and transforming negative thought patterns, such as judgment, criticism, and cynicism, which can hinder our ability to experience love, compassion, and spiritual connection.

Unresolved Karma: Our past and past life actions and unresolved karma can manifest as inner demons that influence our present experiences. Addressing and learning from past mistakes and past life situations or harmful behaviors is a vital aspect of spiritual growth.

Fear and Resistance: Deep-rooted fears, such as fear of change, fear of the unknown, or fear of spiritual awakening, can act as inner demons, holding us back from embracing our true spiritual path.

Spiritual Bypassing: Avoiding or neglecting certain aspects of our spiritual journey by seeking only positive experiences can create inner demons that block authentic growth and self-realization.

Disconnectedness from Soul: Feeling disconnected from the divine or a higher power can lead to feelings of emptiness or spiritual crisis, acting as inner demons that need to be addressed through inner exploration and reconnection.

Spiritual Pride: Over-identification with one's spiritual progress or accomplishments can lead to spiritual pride, which can be an inner demon that blinds us to our own limitations and hinders further growth.

Suppression of Intuition and Inner Guidance: Ignoring or suppressing our inner guidance and intuition can create inner demons that result in confusion and a lack of clarity in our spiritual path.

Spiritual shadow work involves embracing and integrating these inner demons rather than trying to eradicate them. By acknowledging and accepting these aspects of ourselves, we can heal, transform, and elevate our spiritual journey. Engaging in practices like meditation, self-reflection, journaling, prayer, and seeking guidance from spiritual mentors or teachers can be valuable tools for navigating and integrating our spiritual shadow aspects.

The ultimate goal of spiritual shadow work is to move toward a state of greater spiritual wholeness and alignment with our authentic self, leading to a deeper connection with the divine and a sense of purpose and fulfillment in life.

Preventing the ego from becoming an inner demon in spiritual practice requires ongoing awareness, self-reflection, and mindful cultivation of certain qualities. Here are some strategies to keep the ego in check and foster spiritual growth:

Cultivate Humility: Embrace humility and recognize that you are part of a larger interconnected whole. Avoid falling into the trap of spiritual pride or superiority over others.

Non-Attachment: Practice non-attachment to outcomes, beliefs, and identities. The ego often clings to specific ideas or desires, causing suffering when they are not fulfilled.

Observe Egoic Reactions: Develop the ability to observe your egoic reactions without being consumed by them. Mindful awareness allows you to respond consciously instead of reacting impulsively.

Ego Dissolution Practices: Engage in practices that temporarily dissolve the ego's hold on your perception of self, such as meditation, contemplation, or experiences of awe in nature.

Self-Inquiry: Regularly question your beliefs, self-concepts, and motivations. Ask yourself, "Who am I beyond my thoughts and identities?" This self-inquiry can help you uncover the ego's illusions.

Service and Compassion: Focus on serving others with genuine compassion and kindness. Serving selflessly can shift the ego's focus from self-centeredness to the well-being of others.

Gratitude Practice: Cultivate gratitude for life's blessings and acknowledge the contributions of others to your growth and well-being. Gratitude helps counteract ego-driven entitlement.

Stay Open to Feedback: Be open to feedback from others, especially when it pertains to your behavior and attitudes. Accepting constructive criticism can help you identify egoic patterns.

Authenticity: Embrace authenticity and vulnerability. Allow yourself to be honest about your struggles and imperfections, recognizing that they are part of being human.

Detachment from Labels: Avoid overly identifying with labels or titles, such as "spiritual," "enlightened," or "awakened." These labels can reinforce the ego's need for validation and recognition.

Practice Selflessness: Engage in acts of selflessness and kindness without seeking praise or recognition. Acts of selfless service help dissolve the ego's need for external validation.

Maintain a Beginner's Mind: Cultivate a beginner's mind, remaining open and receptive to new insights and perspectives. The ego can become stagnant when it clings to fixed beliefs.

Mindful Consumption: Be mindful of what you consume, whether it's media, information, or material possessions. Avoid feeding the ego with excessive self-focused content.

The ego is a natural and necessary aspect of being human, helping us navigate the world and maintain a sense of individuality. The key is not to suppress the ego but to develop a healthy relationship with it, where it serves as a tool rather than a dominant force in our lives. By staying mindful and cultivating qualities like humility, compassion, and authenticity, you can prevent the ego from becoming an inner demon and allow it to harmoniously coexist with your spiritual journey.

Letting go of attachments and material possessions for spiritual shadow work is a transformative process that requires self-awareness, willingness, and mindful practice. Here are some steps to help you navigate this journey:

Self-Reflection: Begin by reflecting on your attachments and material possessions. Consider why you are attached to certain things and how they may be influencing your sense of self and happiness.

Identify Core Values: Clarify your core values and priorities in life. Focus on what truly matters to you beyond material possessions and external achievements.

Practice Gratitude: Cultivate daily gratitude practice. Acknowledge and appreciate the abundance in your life beyond material possessions, such as relationships, experiences, and personal growth.

Start Small: Begin letting go of attachments gradually. Start with small possessions or less emotionally charged items to build your capacity to release attachments.

Mindfulness and Detachment: Practice mindfulness to observe your attachments without judgment. Cultivate a sense of detachment by recognizing that possessions are impermanent and do not define your true self.

Embrace Minimalism: Consider adopting a minimalist lifestyle. Simplifying your life can help you focus on what truly matters and reduce the emotional weight of material possessions.

Donate and Share: Instead of hoarding possessions, donate or share them with others. This act of generosity can foster a sense of interconnectedness and reduce the hold of attachments.

Question Your Beliefs: Examine the beliefs that fuel your attachments. Challenge assumptions about what brings happiness and fulfillment in life.

Let Go of the Past: Release attachments to possessions that are tied to memories or identities. Embrace the present moment and the person you are becoming.

Seek Experiences over Possessions: Invest more in experiences rather than acquiring material possessions. Experiences often provide more lasting joy and personal growth.

Find Inner Fulfillment: Explore practices that bring inner fulfillment, such as meditation, creative expression, or spending time in nature. Inner contentment reduces the need for external validation.

Practice Self-Compassion: Be kind to yourself during this process. Letting go of attachments can be challenging, and it's normal to experience resistance or ambivalence. Treat yourself with love and patience.

Community and Support: Surround yourself with like-minded individuals or join a community that values spiritual growth and letting go of attachments. Support from others can be encouraging and motivating.

Letting go of negative patterns in spiritual shadow work is a profound and liberating process. It involves exploring your unconscious thoughts, emotions, and behaviors to identify these patterns and then actively working to release their hold on your life. Here are some steps to help you in this transformative journey:

Self-Awareness: Begin by cultivating self-awareness. Pay attention to your thoughts, emotions, and actions throughout your daily life. Notice any recurring negative patterns that arise.

Identify the Root Cause: Try to identify the root cause of these negative patterns. Reflect on your past experiences, traumas, and conditioning that might be contributing to these patterns.

Practice Mindfulness: Engage in mindfulness practices to stay present with your thoughts and emotions without judgment. Mindfulness can help you recognize negative patterns as they arise and create space for conscious responses.

Challenge Negative Beliefs: Question the negative beliefs that underlie these patterns. Are these beliefs based on reality, or are they distortions created by past experiences? Replace them with more positive and empowering beliefs.

Emotional Release: Allow yourself to feel and process any suppressed emotions related to these negative patterns. Cry, scream, or express emotions in a safe and healthy way to release emotional energy.

Seek Support: Don't hesitate to seek support from a therapist, counselor, or spiritual mentor. They can offer valuable guidance and help you navigate the process.

Replace with Positive Habits: Gradually replace negative patterns with positive habits and behaviors. Consistently practicing new behaviors can create new neural pathways in the brain, making positive changes more sustainable.

Inner Dialogue: Engage in an inner dialogue with yourself to understand the deeper motivations behind these negative patterns. Be compassionate and non-judgmental toward yourself during this process.

Forgive Yourself: Forgive yourself for past mistakes and any harm caused by these negative patterns. Self-forgiveness is a crucial step in letting go and moving forward.

Set Intentions: Set clear intentions to let go of these negative patterns and replace them with healthier alternatives. Regularly reaffirm your commitment to personal growth and transformation.

Celebrate Progress: Acknowledge and celebrate your progress, no matter how small it may seem. Each step forward is a testament to your inner strength and determination.

Patience and Perseverance: Spiritual shadow work is an ongoing process, and letting go of negative patterns takes time. Be patient with yourself and persevere, knowing that positive change is possible.

By actively engaging in spiritual shadow work and letting go of negative patterns, you free yourself from the limitations of the past and create space for new possibilities and personal growth. Remember that this is a journey of self-compassion and self-discovery, and with dedication and inner work, you can transform negative patterns and experience greater inner freedom and well-being.

Dealing with unresolved karma in spiritual shadow work can be a powerful process of self-awareness and healing. Unresolved karma refers to the consequences of past actions and experiences that continue to influence your present life. Dealing with unresolved karma from a past life in spiritual shadow work requires a similar approach to addressing current-life karma, but with the added dimension of exploring past-life experiences.

Acceptance and Responsibility: Start by accepting that unresolved karma exists and acknowledging your role in creating it. Take responsibility for your past actions without self-blame or guilt.

Self-Reflection: Engage in deep self-reflection to identify patterns and recurring themes in your life. Look for connections between past actions and current challenges or situations.

Identify Lessons and Growth Opportunities: Consider the lessons and growth opportunities that unresolved karma presents. What can you learn from these experiences, and how can you use them to evolve spiritually?

Compassion for Yourself and Others: Cultivate compassion for yourself and others involved in karmic events. This includes those who may have caused you harm or those you may have hurt in the past.

Forgiveness: Practice forgiveness for yourself and others. This doesn't mean condoning harmful actions but releasing the emotional burden associated with unresolved karma.

Self-Healing Practices: Engage in self-healing practices, such as energy work, Reiki, or other healing modalities, to release blocked energies and emotional wounds associated with unresolved karma.

Seek Guidance from Spiritual Teachers or Mentors: Reach out to spiritual teachers or mentors who can provide guidance and support as you work through unresolved karma.

Karmic Reparation: Consider making amends or reparations when appropriate and possible. This may involve apologizing to someone you've hurt or taking positive actions to counterbalance negative past actions.

Detach from Outcomes: Let go of expectations regarding how resolving unresolved karma should look like. Trust in the process and remain open to whatever unfolds.

Practice Patience: Healing unresolved karma is a gradual process. Practice patience with yourself as you work through past issues and challenges.

Focus on Present Moment: While acknowledging unresolved karma, remember to focus on the present moment. Embrace the opportunities for growth and positive change in your current life.

Openness to Past-Life Exploration: Approach the concept of past lives with an open mind. Be willing to explore the idea that unresolved karma may have its roots in experiences from previous lifetimes.

Regression Therapy or Past-Life Meditation: Consider engaging in regression therapy or past-life meditation to access past-life memories and experiences. This can provide insights into the unresolved karma you are currently facing.

Dream Analysis: Pay attention to recurring dreams or vivid dreams that may offer glimpses into past-life experiences. Analyzing these dreams can reveal valuable information about unresolved karma.

Meditation and Visualization: Practice meditation and visualization to connect with your higher self or spiritual guides. Ask for guidance and understanding about any unresolved karma you may be carrying from past lives.

Karmic Patterns: Look for patterns or recurring themes in your current life that may indicate unresolved karma. These patterns could be related to relationships, challenges, or unexplained emotions.

Acceptance and Non-Judgment: Approach past-life karma with acceptance and non-judgment. Avoid blaming yourself or others for past actions, as this can hinder the healing process.

Self-Compassion: Offer yourself self-compassion and kindness as you explore and confront past-life karma. Remember that healing is a gradual process that requires patience and understanding.

Forgiveness and Releasing Attachments: Practice forgiveness for yourself and others involved in past-life karmic events. Release any attachments or negative emotions connected to those experiences.

Learning the Lessons: Seek to understand the lessons and growth opportunities presented by past-life karma. How can you apply these lessons to your current life for personal development?

Healing Modalities: Engage in healing modalities that can help release past-life traumas and energy blockages. Energy healing, Reiki, or other practices can assist in clearing unresolved karma.

Integration and Transformation: Work on integrating the insights gained from past-life exploration into your current life. Seek ways to transform any negative karmic patterns into positive actions and behaviors.

Trust the Process: Trust that the process of addressing past-life karma is unfolding as it should. Have faith in your spiritual journey and the wisdom it brings.

Balancing the Present: While exploring past-life karma, don't neglect your current-life responsibilities and opportunities. Focus on balancing spiritual growth with practical actions in your daily life.

Understanding when it comes to past life might be a shadow that affects us but is not one that is present in our current life. To deal with past life shadows we need to address the one we are currently living with and understand that the ones in the past will appear in this lifetime as lessons for the soul.

Fear and resistance in spiritual shadow work is essential for making progress in your inner exploration and healing. Fear and resistance are natural reactions to confronting deep-seated emotions and aspects of yourself that have been repressed or denied. Here are some strategies to help you navigate fear and resistance in your spiritual shadow work:

Acknowledge and Accept: Start by acknowledging that fear and resistance are normal parts of the process. Accept that these feelings are present and allow yourself to feel them without judgment.

Create a Safe Space: Establish a safe and supportive environment for your shadow work. Choose a quiet and comfortable space where you can explore your emotions and thoughts without distractions.

Start Slowly: Begin with smaller, less intimidating aspects of your shadow before delving into more profound issues. Gradually build your comfort level with the process.

Mindful Awareness: Practice mindful awareness when fear and resistance arise. Observe these emotions without getting caught up in their intensity. Use your breath as an anchor to stay present.

Self-Compassion: Be compassionate with yourself during the shadow work process. Understand that facing the unknown can be challenging, and it's okay to experience fear and resistance.

Inner Dialogue: Engage in an inner dialogue with yourself. Ask yourself why you feel fear or resistance and what might be the underlying causes of these emotions.

Seek Support: Talk to a trusted friend, mentor, or therapist about your experiences with fear and resistance. Having someone to share your journey can provide encouragement and validation.

Visualizations and Guided Meditations: Use visualizations or guided meditations specifically designed to address fear and resistance in shadow work. These practices can help you work through the emotions in a supportive way.

Break It Down: Break down the shadow work into smaller, manageable steps. Each step you take can build your confidence and reduce the impact of fear and resistance.

Set Intentions: Set clear intentions for your shadow work, focusing on growth and healing. Remind yourself of the benefits of facing your shadows and moving towards self-awareness.

Embrace Vulnerability: Embrace the vulnerability that comes with shadow work. It takes courage to confront your inner demons, but it can lead to profound transformation and growth.

Celebrate Progress: Celebrate your progress, no matter how small it may seem. Each step you take in confronting fear and resistance is a significant achievement.

Remember that fear and resistance are normal aspects of the spiritual shadow work process. Embrace them as opportunities for growth and deeper self-understanding. As you work through these emotions, you'll find that the healing and insights gained are well worth the effort. Be patient with yourself and trust in your ability to navigate your inner landscape with courage and grace.

Spiritual bypassing in spiritual shadow work is crucial for ensuring that your inner exploration is authentic, honest, and transformative. Spiritual bypassing is when individuals use spiritual beliefs or practices to avoid facing and healing unresolved emotional or psychological issues. Here are some strategies to help you recognize and address spiritual bypassing in your spiritual shadow work:

Develop Self-Awareness: Cultivate self-awareness to recognize when you might be using spiritual practices to bypass difficult emotions or unresolved issues.

Pay attention to any tendencies to "spiritualize" away your challenges.

Honest Self-Reflection: Engage in honest self-reflection about your motivations for spiritual practices. Ask yourself if you are using them as a distraction or to escape from facing your shadows.

Examine Your Intentions: Be honest with yourself about why you are drawn to spirituality and shadow work. Are you genuinely seeking growth and healing, or are you seeking validation or escape?

Embrace Vulnerability: Allow yourself to be vulnerable and authentic in your spiritual journey. Acknowledge your struggles and challenges without judgment or self-criticism.

Avoid Spiritually Superior Attitudes: Be mindful of any tendencies to feel spiritually superior to others. Remember that everyone is on their unique path, and there is no hierarchy in personal growth.

Stay Grounded: Ground yourself in the present moment and your physical reality. Avoid using spirituality to dissociate from your emotions or daily life.

Work with a Therapist or Guide: If you find it challenging to navigate your shadows on your own, consider working with a therapist or spiritual guide. They can provide support and help you stay accountable in your healing journey.

Balance Light and Dark: Embrace both the light and dark aspects of your being. Spiritual growth involves integrating all parts of yourself, including the shadows.

Practice Mindfulness: Practice mindfulness to stay present with your emotions and experiences. Mindfulness helps you avoid bypassing uncomfortable emotions by staying with them non-judgmentally.

Shadow Work Exercises: Engage in specific shadow work exercises that encourage you to face and explore your shadows. This might include journaling, inner dialogue, or creative expression.

Release Expectations: Let go of expectations about how your spiritual journey should unfold. Be open to surprises, challenges, and moments of uncertainty.

Embrace Emotional Healing: Embrace emotional healing as an essential part of your spiritual journey. Don't shy away from difficult emotions but allow yourself to feel and process them.

Be Patient with Yourself: Spiritual shadow work is a process that takes time and patience. Be kind to yourself and celebrate the progress you make, no matter how small.

By addressing spiritual bypassing and embracing the true depth of your spiritual shadow work, you create a space for profound healing, self-discovery, and genuine spiritual growth. Remember that this journey is about integration and wholeness, embracing all aspects of yourself, both light and shadow.

The disconnectedness of the soul in spiritual shadow work involves delving deep into the root causes of this disconnection and working to heal and integrate the fragmented aspects of your being. Not knowing who you are and how you feel is one of the hardest feelings to have to confront and explore. Not knowing where we come from, where we are going and not having a core of belief can definitely affect this kind of healing. This is not about religion or deity; this is about you and what you believe about you on a soul level.

Here are specific steps to address the disconnectedness of the soul through spiritual shadow work:

Acceptance and Acknowledgment: Begin by accepting and acknowledging the feelings of disconnectedness without judgment. Understand that these feelings are valid and are part of your spiritual journey.

Inner Exploration: Engage in introspection and inner exploration to identify the underlying beliefs, traumas, or experiences that have contributed to the disconnection of your soul. This might involve journaling, meditation, or therapeutic practices.

Uncover Repressed Emotions: Explore any repressed or suppressed emotions that may be hindering your soul's connection. Allow yourself to feel and process these emotions in a safe and supportive way.

Self-Compassion: Be gentle and compassionate with yourself throughout the process. Treat yourself as you would a dear friend going through a challenging time.

Seek Support: Consider seeking support from a therapist, spiritual mentor, or counselor who can guide you through the process of spiritual shadow work and provide insights and encouragement.

Practice Mindfulness: Practice mindfulness to become aware of your thoughts, emotions, and sensations as they arise. Mindfulness can help you stay present with your experiences and reconnect with your inner self.

Inner Dialogue: Engage in an inner dialogue with your disconnected aspects. Ask them what they need and what messages they have for you. Listen to your inner wisdom with an open heart.

Reconnect with Nature: Spend time in nature to foster a sense of grounding and connection with the natural world. Nature can be a powerful catalyst for soul connection.

Express Your Authentic Self: Embrace your authentic self and express it without fear of judgment. Allow yourself to be vulnerable and genuine in your interactions with others.

Practice Gratitude and Appreciation: Cultivate gratitude for the blessings in your life and appreciate the lessons that disconnection has brought you. Gratitude can shift your perspective and open your heart.

Healing Rituals: Engage in healing rituals or practices that resonate with you. This could include energy healing, sound healing, or other modalities that help release blocked energy and facilitate soul connection.

Integration and Alignment: Work on integrating the insights gained from your shadow work into your daily life. Align your thoughts, behaviors, and actions with your soul's true essence.

By engaging in spiritual shadow work, you can bring to light the aspects of your soul that have been disconnected and begin the process of healing and integration. Embrace this journey as an opportunity for self-discovery and growth, and remember that by addressing the disconnectedness of your soul, you can experience a deeper sense of inner peace, purpose, and spiritual connection.

Chapter 5 Forgiveness and Self-Compassion:

Spiritual forgiveness is a concept that relates to the act of forgiving someone or oneself from a spiritual or religious perspective. It goes beyond the mere act of letting go of anger or resentment and involves a deeper understanding of human interconnectedness, compassion, and the recognition of a higher power or divine presence.

Transcendence: Spiritual forgiveness often involves transcending ego-based thoughts and emotions. It goes beyond the desire for revenge or retaliation and seeks to rise above negative memories by connecting to a higher, more compassionate state of being. Understanding that a feeling is not negative but where it comes from or who is coming from, is not revenge what you seek but the release of those emotional ties that hold you back and are controlling your life. We need to feel it to be able to experience spiritual forgiveness.

Spiritual/Self-forgiveness is crucial in spiritual shadow work for several important reasons:

Compassion and Healing: Shadow work involves exploring and acknowledging the parts of ourselves that we may have suppressed, denied, or judged negatively. Self-forgiveness allows us to extend compassion to ourselves and embrace our imperfections and mistakes with kindness and understanding. This compassionate approach is essential for healing and transforming the wounded aspects of our psyche and spirit. Practicing spiritual forgiveness involves cultivating a deep sense of compassion and empathy, both towards oneself and others. Understanding that all beings are interconnected and share the human experience helps to foster a greater sense of forgiveness.

Compassion and healing in spiritual shadow work is essential for creating a safe and supportive environment for your inner exploration and growth. Here are some practical steps to incorporate compassion and healing into your shadow work practice:

Non-judgmental awareness: Approach your shadow work with an attitude of non-judgmental awareness. Recognize that everyone has a shadow, and it is a natural part of being human. Be gentle with yourself and avoid self-criticism when uncovering challenging aspects of yourself.

Cultivate self-compassion: Treat yourself with kindness and understanding. When you encounter difficult emotions or uncover aspects of yourself you don't like, offer yourself compassion and self-forgiveness. Remember that you are doing this work to heal and grow, not to further criticize yourself.

Create a safe space: Find a quiet and comfortable space where you can engage in your shadow work without distractions or interruptions. This safe environment will allow you to fully explore your emotions and experiences without feeling vulnerable.

Meditation and mindfulness: Practice meditation or mindfulness to observe your thoughts and emotions without attachment. Mindfulness can help you stay present and grounded during challenging moments in your shadow work.

Inner child work: Often, our shadows are connected to unresolved childhood experiences. Engaging in inner child work can help you address past wounds and offer healing and understanding to your younger self.

Creative expression: Engage in creative activities like art, writing, dance, or music to express your emotions and experiences. Creativity can be a powerful outlet for healing and processing your shadow aspects.

Integrate and transmute: As you uncover and understand your shadow aspects, work on integrating them into your conscious awareness. Accept and embrace these parts of yourself with love and compassion. Transform any negative or destructive patterns into positive and constructive behaviors.

Self-care: Take care of yourself physically, emotionally, and spiritually. Engage in activities that nourish and support your well-being. Self-care is an essential aspect of the healing process.

Breaking Cycles of Shame and Guilt: When we carry shame and guilt from past actions or unresolved issues, they can perpetuate negative patterns and self-sabotaging behaviors. Self-forgiveness breaks these cycles by releasing the emotional burden, allowing us to move forward with greater freedom and self-acceptance. I believe a deeper understanding about patterns and cycles are not the same for spiritual shadow work.

In the context of spiritual shadow work, patterns and cycles are related concepts but not the same thing.

Patterns refer to recurring themes, behaviors, or thought processes that are often unconscious and deeply ingrained within an individual. These patterns are formed through past experiences, beliefs, conditioning, and unresolved emotions. In the realm of shadow work, identifying these patterns is crucial because they may be linked to unresolved issues or aspects of the self that have been repressed or denied.

Shadow work involves bringing these patterns into conscious awareness, exploring their origins, and understanding how they impact one's thoughts, emotions, and actions. By acknowledging and integrating these shadow aspects, individuals can experience healing, personal growth, and greater self-awareness.

On the other hand, cycles in spiritual shadow work refer to repetitive sequences of events or experiences that may occur in one's life. These cycles can be linked to unresolved patterns and may serve as opportunities for growth and transformation. Cycles might involve repeated challenges, conflicts, or situations that trigger specific emotional responses.

Recognizing cycles in shadow work allows individuals to discern the lessons they are meant to learn and the areas of their lives that require attention and healing. Breaking free from negative cycles often involves consciously choosing different responses and actions, which can lead to a more empowered and authentic way of living.

Shadow work involves bringing these patterns into conscious awareness, exploring their origins, and understanding how they impact one's thoughts, emotions, and actions. By acknowledging and integrating these shadow aspects, individuals can experience healing, personal growth, and greater self-awareness.

On the other hand, cycles in spiritual shadow work refer to repetitive sequences of events or experiences that may occur in one's life. These cycles can be linked to unresolved patterns and may serve as opportunities for growth and transformation. Cycles might involve repeated challenges, conflicts, or situations that trigger specific emotional responses.

Recognizing cycles in shadow work allows individuals to discern the lessons they are meant to learn and the areas of their lives that require attention and healing. Breaking free from negative cycles often involves consciously choosing different responses and actions, which can lead to a more empowered and authentic way of living.

In summary, patterns and cycles are interconnected in spiritual shadow work, but they represent different aspects of the inner work process. Identifying and understanding patterns helps to shed light on unconscious behaviors and beliefs, while recognizing cycles provides insight into the repetitive nature of certain life experiences and the potential for transformation. Both aspects play a significant role in the journey of self-discovery and healing in shadow work.

Integration and Wholeness: The goal of shadow work is to integrate the hidden aspects of ourselves into our conscious awareness. Self-forgiveness paves the way for this integration by accepting all parts of ourselves, including the aspects we may have deemed unacceptable. Embracing our shadow with forgiveness contributes to a sense of wholeness and self-empowerment.

It is a fundamental goal in shadow work. The process of shadow work involves acknowledging and embracing the disowned or suppressed aspects of oneself (the "shadow") to achieve a more balanced and authentic sense of self. Here's how integration and wholeness play a role in this transformative journey:

Acknowledging the Shadow: The first step in shadow work is recognizing that everyone has a shadow – a collection of aspects, emotions, desires, and beliefs that are hidden from our conscious awareness. Integration begins with acknowledging the existence of these aspects without denial or judgment.

Exploring the Shadow: Once the shadow is acknowledged, the next step is to explore its contents. This involves delving into past experiences, examining beliefs, patterns, and behaviors that have been repressed or denied. The exploration allows you to gain a deeper understanding of your unconscious motivations and reactions.

Acceptance and Compassion: Integration requires acceptance and compassion for the parts of yourself that you discover during your shadow work. Rather than rejecting or condemning these aspects, approach them with understanding and kindness. Remember that these parts are a natural and integral aspect of being human.

Healing Past Wounds: Shadow work often uncovers unresolved traumas and wounds from the past. Integrating these experiences involves healing and processing the emotions associated with them, allowing you to release the hold they may have on your present life.

Embracing the Whole Self: The aim of shadow work is not to eliminate the shadow but to integrate it into your conscious awareness. Embrace all aspects of yourself, including the shadow, as part of the rich tapestry of your being. This integration leads to a more authentic and complete sense of self.

Transforming Negative Patterns: Integrating the shadow involves recognizing negative patterns and behaviors that arise from the shadow aspects. By bringing them into conscious awareness, you can work on transforming these patterns into healthier, more constructive ways of being.

Embodying Wholeness: As you integrate your shadow, you begin to experience a sense of wholeness within yourself.

Embracing both your light and shadow sides allows you to feel more grounded, balanced, and at peace with yourself.

Aligning with Higher Self: Shadow work is also about aligning with your higher self or true essence. By integrating the shadow, you remove the barriers that may prevent you from connecting with your authentic nature and living in alignment with your values and purpose.

Empathy and Understanding: As you integrate your shadow, you become more empathetic and understanding towards others. Recognizing your own vulnerabilities and imperfections allows you to extend the same compassion to others, fostering deeper connections and relationships.

Empowerment and Personal Growth: Self-forgiveness empowers us to take responsibility for our actions and choices while acknowledging that we are not defined solely by our mistakes. By releasing self-blame, we create space for personal growth, allowing us to learn from our experiences and make positive changes in our lives.

Cultivating Self-Love: Forgiving ourselves cultivates self-love and self-compassion. As we show ourselves the same kindness and understanding we would offer to a loved one, we strengthen our relationship with ourselves and develop a deeper sense of self-worth.

Embracing Imperfection: Shadow work helps us understand that being human means being imperfect. Through self-forgiveness, we embrace our humanness and recognize that growth and transformation involve accepting our flaws and imperfections.

Releasing Emotional Baggage: Carrying unresolved guilt or self-condemnation can be a heavy emotional burden that hinders our progress and spiritual development. Self-forgiveness lifts this weight, allowing us to move forward with a lighter heart and an open mind.

Enhancing Spiritual Connection: Forgiveness is often considered a spiritual virtue in many belief systems. Engaging in self-forgiveness aligns us with higher spiritual principles, fostering a deeper connection to our spirituality and our understanding of the interconnectedness of all beings.

Forgive yourself for past actions or judgments related to your shadow aspects. Embrace self-compassion and recognize that everyone has a shadow, and it is a natural part of being human.

Ritualistic Actions: Some shadow integration rituals may involve symbolic actions, such as burning pieces of paper with written fears or negative beliefs, releasing them to the universe as a way of letting go.

Journaling and Integration: After the ritual, take time to journal about your experience. Record any insights, emotions, or revelations that emerged during the process. Continue to reflect on your shadow work and integrate the lessons learned into your daily life.

Embrace the Lessons: Recognize that the shadow self holds valuable lessons and insights. When you confront and integrate these aspects, you gain a deeper understanding of yourself and others. Embrace the growth and wisdom that arise from the process.

Transcend Duality: Embracing the dark mirror involves transcending the dualistic view of good and bad, light and dark. Instead, recognize that both light and shadow aspects are part of the totality of your being. Embrace the wholeness of your nature and embrace the unity within yourself.

Seek Guidance and Support: If you encounter significant emotional challenges or find it difficult to navigate the process on your own, seek guidance and support from spiritual teachers, mentors, or therapists experienced in shadow work and spiritual growth.

Practice Surrender and Letting Go: Release attachment to the need to control or suppress certain emotions or aspects of yourself. Surrender to the process of embracing the dark mirror, trusting that it will lead to greater self-awareness and spiritual evolution.

Express Gratitude: Be grateful for the opportunity to embark on this journey of self-discovery and growth. Embracing the dark mirror is an act of courage and love towards yourself, and it opens the door to deeper spiritual insights and understanding.

Self-Acceptance: Accepting that you, like all humans, have both light and shadow aspects is the first step. Embrace the idea that the shadow self is an inherent part of being human, and it does not define your worth or value as a person.

Self-Exploration: Engage in introspective practices like journaling, meditation, or therapy to explore the depths of your subconscious. Delve into your thoughts, emotions, and past experiences to identify patterns and recurring themes.

Facing Fears: Confronting your fears and uncomfortable emotions can be challenging, but it is essential for growth. Avoiding or suppressing these feelings only strengthens their hold on you. Embrace the discomfort and allow yourself to experience and process these emotions.

Compassion for Yourself: Be kind and compassionate towards yourself during this journey. Avoid self-judgment and self-criticism. Remember that healing and growth take time, and it is okay to take small steps towards embracing your shadow.

Integration: Embracing the shadow self is not about getting rid of these aspects but integrating them into your whole self. Recognize that these hidden parts carry valuable lessons and potential for growth. By integrating the shadow, you can harness its energy positively and avoid projecting it onto others.

Embracing Wholeness: Embracing the dark mirror of the shadow self is ultimately about embracing your wholeness. By accepting and integrating all parts of yourself, you become a more authentic and empowered individual.

Chapter 6: Embracing the Sacred Wounds

Spiritual sacred wounds are emotional and psychological wounds that hold deep spiritual significance and potential for growth and transformation on a soul level. These wounds are not just ordinary painful experiences but are viewed as sacred because of their potential to lead individuals to higher levels of consciousness, self-awareness, and spiritual awakening.

Spiritual sacred wounds may include:

Dark Night of the Soul: A profound and challenging spiritual experience marked by feelings of spiritual emptiness, disconnection, and a crisis of faith.

Loss of Belief Systems: When individuals experience a shift or loss of previously held belief systems, it can lead to a sense of confusion and existential questioning.

Spiritual Awakening Experiences: Intense spiritual experiences that can be overwhelming and disorienting, such as sudden insights, visions, or altered states of consciousness.

Kundalini Awakening: An energetic awakening that involves the rising of spiritual energy, which can be intense and transformative.

Spiritual Betrayal: Feeling betrayed or disillusioned by spiritual teachers, teachings, or communities, leading to spiritual wounds and loss of trust.

Soul Contracts and Lessons: The recognition and understanding of karmic or soul contracts that involve challenging relationships or life circumstances for the purpose of spiritual growth.

Existential Questions: Deep existential questions about the nature of life, death, and the universe, which can lead to a sense of existential angst.

Transpersonal Crisis: Intense psychological and spiritual experiences that challenge one's understanding of reality and self-identity.

Healing Abilities and Responsibility: The awakening of spiritual or healing abilities that come with the responsibility to use them ethically and compassionately.

Near-Death Experiences: Profound encounters with death that can lead to significant shifts in beliefs and values.

Past Life Memories: Recollections of past lives that may bring up unresolved emotions or traumas from previous incarnations.

Empathic Sensitivity: Heightened empathic sensitivity, leading to the absorption of collective or others' emotional energies.

Feeling Disconnected from Soul: A sense of disconnection from the Divine or the feeling of being spiritually lost.

When combined with life experiences this brings deeper pain and deeper disconnection to us on a spiritual level but also on a mundane one. Here are some other examples of how our daily lives can be affected.

Trauma: Traumatic events, such as physical or emotional abuse, accidents, or significant losses, can leave deep wounds that have lasting effects.

Betrayal: Experiences of betrayal, whether in personal relationships or professional settings, can create wounds that affect trust and self-worth.

Rejection and Abandonment: Experiencing rejection or abandonment by loved ones can leave profound wounds that impact one's sense of belonging and self-value.

Loss and Grief: The loss of a loved one or significant life changes can lead to wounds associated with grief and mourning.

Shame and Guilt: Feelings of shame or guilt resulting from past actions or experiences can become deep-seated wounds that affect self-esteem and self-acceptance.

Identity Crisis: Experiences that challenge or disrupt a person's sense of identity and purpose can create wounds related to self-discovery and self-acceptance.

Spiritual sacred wounds are seen as opportunities for soul growth, self-realization, and alignment with one's spiritual path. Embracing and working with these wounds can lead to profound spiritual insights, deep healing, and a sense of unity with the larger cosmic consciousness. However, the process of working with spiritual sacred wounds requires patience, self-compassion, and a willingness to explore the depths of one's being. Seeking support from experienced spiritual guides, mentors, or therapists can be beneficial on this transformative journey.

Embracing the sacred wounds in spiritual shadow work is a powerful and transformative process that involves acknowledging and honoring the deeper significance of your wounds. Sacred wounds are the emotional and psychological wounds that hold profound meaning and potential for growth and healing. Here's how to approach embracing sacred wounds in your spiritual shadow work:

Cultivate Self-Compassion: Approach your wounds with self-compassion and understanding. Recognize that these wounds are a natural part of the human experience, and you are not defined by them.

Explore the Stories Behind the Wounds: Dive deep into the stories and experiences that led to your wounds. Understand the root causes and the impact they have had on your life.

Acceptance and Non-Judgment: Practice acceptance and non-judgment towards your wounds. Embrace them as part of your journey and learning experiences.

Mindful Awareness: Stay mindfully aware of how your wounds manifest in your thoughts, emotions, and behaviors. Mindfulness can help you gain insights into their effects on your life.

Inner Child Work: Connect with your inner child and explore how your wounds may have originated during your early years. Offer love and healing to your inner child to facilitate growth.

Emotional Release: Allow yourself to feel and express the emotions associated with your wounds. Release any pent-up emotions through healthy outlets like journaling, art, or talking to a supportive friend or therapist.

Recognize the Gifts: Explore the gifts and strengths that have emerged from your wounds. Sacred wounds often carry profound lessons and opportunities for personal growth and resilience.

Forgiveness: Practice forgiveness towards yourself and others involved in the wounds. Forgiveness can liberate you from carrying the burden of past pain.

Embrace Vulnerability: Embrace vulnerability as you confront your wounds. Being vulnerable opens you to deeper healing and connection with yourself and others.

Transmute the Energy: Channel the energy from your wounds into creative or transformative pursuits. Use your experiences to create positive change and contribute to your personal growth.

Integration: Integrate the lessons and insights gained from working with your sacred wounds into your daily life. Apply this knowledge to make healthier choices and foster personal growth.

Soul Connection: Connect with your soul to understand the spiritual significance of your wounds. See how they are guiding you towards higher levels of consciousness and self-awareness.

Gratitude and Blessings: Cultivate gratitude for the growth and wisdom gained from embracing your sacred wounds. See them as blessings that have shaped your journey.

Here is a ritual to help you embrace your sacred wounds:

Preparation:

Choose a quiet and sacred space where you can perform the ritual without interruptions.

Gather items that hold spiritual significance to you, such as crystals, candles, incense, or objects from nature.

Have a journal and pen nearby to write down any insights or feelings that arise during the ritual.

Steps:

Setting Intentions: Begin by setting clear intentions for the ritual. Reflect on your desire to embrace and honor your spiritual sacred wounds as gateways to growth and transformation.

Creating Sacred Space: Light a candle or incense to symbolize the presence of the Divine or higher consciousness. Take a few deep breaths to center yourself and create a sacred space within and around you.

Invocation: Call upon any spiritual guides, deities, or higher powers that resonate with you to support and guide you through the process.

Recalling the Wounds: Take some time to reflect on the spiritual sacred wounds you have experienced. Allow yourself to feel the emotions and memories associated with these wounds without judgment.

Petition: Write down your reflections and feelings related to the wounds on a piece of paper. Use this space to express any emotions, insights, or thoughts that arise.

Symbolic Release: Choose an object or representation that symbolizes your spiritual sacred wounds. Hold it in your hands and imbue it with the emotions and experiences associated with the wounds.

Healing Affirmations: Speak healing affirmations or prayers that affirm your willingness to embrace and heal from these wounds. Affirm your commitment to self-compassion and growth.

Surrender and Letting Go: Visualize releasing the emotional weight of these wounds. Imagine them being transformed into light and dissolving into the universe, freeing you from their heavy burden.

Gratitude and Integration: Express gratitude for the lessons and growth that have come from your spiritual sacred wounds. Recognize the wisdom and strength you have gained through these experiences.

Self-Compassion: Offer yourself words of love, forgiveness, and self-compassion. Acknowledge the courage it takes to embrace your wounds and the depth of your own inner strength.

Closing and Grounding: Thank any spiritual guides or higher powers you invoked at the beginning of the ritual. Take a few moments to ground yourself by connecting with the earth beneath you.

Integration into Daily Life: As you go about your day, carry the insights and healing energy from the ritual with you. Embrace your spiritual sacred wounds as part of your journey, knowing that they are sacred gateways to transformation.

This ritual is a personal and sacred practice. Feel free to modify it in any way that feels authentic to you. Allow yourself to be fully present and open to the healing and transformation that can arise from embracing your spiritual sacred wounds with love and acceptance.

You as an individual hold the power to do this, I understand that is difficult and we can always have an excuse why not to do it. If you are in grief, pain or any other emotion that is affecting negatively. Trust me just feeling this was and living life like this proves how strong you are. I believe in you!

Chapter 7: Unraveling the Influence: Transcending Dualities

Embrace the inner part of light and dark within us, finding the harmony and balance that lead us to a better and complete of who we are. Transcending dualities in spiritual shadow work involves moving beyond the concept of "good" or "bad," "light" or "dark," and embracing the idea that all aspects of ourselves are interconnected and valid. It's about acknowledging and integrating both the positive and negative aspects of our personality, emotions, and experiences. Transcending dualities is a profound aspect of spiritual shadow work that leads to a greater sense of inner peace, wholeness, and interconnectedness with all of existence. As you explore the integration of your light and shadow aspects, you open yourself up to new dimensions of self-awareness and spiritual growth. Be patient and compassionate with yourself during this transformative process.

Shame can be experienced through various dualities, creating complex and challenging emotions and beliefs. It is essential to address these dualities of shame with self-compassion, understanding, and non-judgment. Embracing the full range of human experiences and recognizing that everyone faces moments of shame can lead to healing and greater spiritual growth. By bringing shame into the light of awareness, we can transform it into an opportunity for self-acceptance, self-love, and spiritual expansion. There are aspects of us that we feel ashamed of because of society, cultural background, spiritual belief and the things that we like or don't like. To understand that we are unique and different can help in this process of self-evaluation and help us understand that we need to also accept and integrate those shadows back to us. Here are some common dualities of shame in spiritual shadow work:

Light and Dark Aspects: Shame can arise from the belief that one should only embody positive or "light" qualities, leading to a denial or repression of the "darker" aspects of oneself. This duality prevents the full acceptance of one's humanity and authentic self.

Worthiness and Unworthiness: Shame often creates a sense of unworthiness, feeling undeserving of love, acceptance, or spiritual growth. The duality of worthiness and unworthiness can be a significant obstacle to self-compassion and spiritual progress.

Judgment and Compassion: The duality of judgment and compassion arises when we harshly judge ourselves for past actions or perceived flaws, rather than offering ourselves understanding and self-compassion.

Fear and Courage: Shame can breed fear of being vulnerable and exposing our perceived imperfections. This fear can hinder the courage needed to confront and heal shame in spiritual shadow work.

Concealment and Vulnerability: The duality of concealing our shame and embracing vulnerability creates a struggle between maintaining a facade of perfection and opening to authentic healing and growth.

Conditional and Unconditional Love: Shame often leads to the belief that love and acceptance are conditional based on meeting certain expectations or standards. The duality of conditional and unconditional love affects how we perceive and receive love, both from ourselves and others.

Dark Night of the Soul and Spiritual Awakening: Shame can arise during the dark night of the soul—a period of deep spiritual crisis. The duality of feeling spiritually lost and experiencing spiritual awakening creates a challenging internal conflict.

Victimhood and Empowerment: Shame may keep individuals stuck in a victim mentality, feeling powerless to change or heal. Transcending this duality involves embracing empowerment and taking responsibility for personal growth.

Humility and Ego: Shame can blur the line between healthy humility and a negative self-concept, making it challenging to maintain a balanced perspective of oneself.

Purity and Impurity: Shame can create a dichotomy of purity and impurity, making individuals feel tainted or unclean due to past actions or experiences.

Here are some ways to transcend dualities in your spiritual shadow work:

Awareness of Polarities: Recognize that life is full of polarities and contrasts. Embrace the idea that both light and shadow exist within you and within all aspects of life.

Non-Judgmental Observation: Practice observing your thoughts, emotions, and behaviors without judgment. Allow yourself to witness your shadow aspects with compassion and curiosity.

Balancing Opposites: Seek balance between opposing aspects of your personality. For example, if you tend to be overly controlling, explore ways to embrace spontaneity and flexibility.

Integration: Embrace the process of integrating your shadow aspects into your conscious awareness. Understand that acknowledging and accepting them leads to greater wholeness.

Transcend Labels: Release the need to label experiences or emotions as purely positive or negative. Instead, view them as opportunities for growth and learning.

Self-Reflection: Engage in regular self-reflection to identify patterns of thinking or behavior that might be influenced by dualistic thinking.

Mindfulness Practice: Cultivate mindfulness to stay present and non-reactive to dualistic thoughts and emotions. Practice observing thoughts without attaching to them.

Embrace Paradox: Recognize that life is full of paradoxes and contradictions. Embrace the mystery and complexity of existence.

Compassion for All Aspects: Cultivate compassion for both your light and shadow aspects. Treat yourself with the same kindness you would offer to others.

Explore Unity Consciousness: Explore practices that foster unity consciousness, such as meditation, nature connection, or acts of service that dissolve the sense of separation.

Dissolving Ego Identification: Transcend the ego's need to identify with particular traits or labels. Recognize that you are more than any single aspect of yourself.

Celebrate Diversity: Embrace the diversity and multiplicity of life. See the beauty in the richness of experiences and perspectives.

Inner Alchemy: Engage in inner alchemy, where you transform your understanding of dualities into a deeper appreciation of the oneness that underlies all existence.

These quotes, these words have meaning, use them embrace them transcend your duality by accepting who you are. This is a gift from me to you.

"Like the moon and the sun, I embrace the ebb and flow of life, transcending the illusions of duality and dancing in the eternal cosmic rhythm."

"In the tapestry of existence, I am both the weaver and the woven, embracing the threads of light and shadow to create my unique masterpiece."

"Through the prism of my soul, I see the spectrum of colors blending seamlessly, reminding me that unity lies within the embrace of all shades."

"Transcending dualities, I find strength in vulnerability, wisdom in uncertainty, and grace in imperfection."

"Like a butterfly emerging from its cocoon, I break free from the confines of duality, soaring with wings of acceptance and self-discovery."

"In the sacred temple of my heart, I honor the divinity of both joy and sorrow, knowing they are guides on my journey to enlightenment."

"I am the phoenix reborn from ashes, transforming the fires of pain and pleasure into the flames of rebirth and transcendence."

"Embracing the Yin and Yang within, I find the equilibrium that brings harmony to my soul's symphony."

"I dance with the shadows, knowing they are the canvas upon which the light of my soul creates its masterpiece."

"Transcending dualities, I embrace the paradoxes of life, and in their mystery, I find the keys to unlock my infinite potential."

"I am a river flowing through valleys and mountains, merging with both calmness and turbulence, for within this flow, I discover my true essence."

"From the depths of my soul, I rise like a lotus, blossoming in the mud of life, knowing that true beauty is found in the union of all elements."

"In the union of the caterpillar and the butterfly, I learn that transformation requires embracing the entirety of my being, even the parts once deemed insignificant."

"Embracing my Yin and Yang, I find serenity in the dance of opposites, knowing they are the yin-yang map guiding me toward wholeness."

"I am the phoenix in flight, transcending the limits of duality, soaring to the heavens with wings of resilience and liberation."

Spiritual epiphanies can trigger duality, some people call it awakening or an extreme state of self-awareness. A spiritual epiphany will trigger or intensify the experience of duality. A spiritual epiphany is a profound moment of insight, realization, or awakening that can lead to a deep transformation in a person's understanding of themselves and the world around them. However, this transformative experience can also bring to light various dualities and internal conflicts that may have been previously unconscious or unacknowledged. How can this experience cause duality?

Conflict Between Old and New Beliefs: A spiritual epiphany can challenge long-held beliefs and ideologies, leading to an internal conflict between the old belief systems and the newfound realizations. This clash can create a sense of duality within the individual's mind.

Integration of Light and Shadow Aspects: A spiritual epiphany may bring awareness to both the light and shadow aspects of one's personality and experiences. The recognition of these dualities can be confronting and necessitate integration and self-acceptance.

Sense of Ego Dissolution: During a spiritual epiphany, individuals may experience a sense of ego dissolution or transcendence. This can lead to a conflict between the ego's desire for identity and the spiritual understanding of interconnectedness.

Balancing Spiritual Insights with Daily Life: Integrating profound spiritual insights into daily life can be challenging. The contrast between the spiritual experience and the practical aspects of life may create a sense of duality.

Attachment and Detachment: A spiritual epiphany may evoke a desire for detachment from materialistic pursuits and attachments. However, the attachment to this newfound understanding itself can create a duality.

Desire for Perfection: After experiencing a spiritual epiphany, individuals may strive for a state of perfection or enlightenment, which can create a duality between their current state and an idealized version of themselves.

Navigating the Spiritual Journey: A spiritual epiphany can open a path of continuous growth and exploration. The journey may involve navigating dualities between moments of clarity and moments of uncertainty or spiritual progress and regress.

Integration of Unity and Diversity: Spiritual epiphanies often highlight the interconnectedness of all existence. However, individuals may struggle with the duality of embracing unity while also celebrating the diversity and individuality of life.

While a spiritual epiphany can lead to a deeper understanding of the interconnected nature of reality, it can also trigger various dualities that are essential aspects of human experience. Embracing these dualities with self-awareness, self-compassion, and a willingness to explore their lessons can lead to further growth and integration on the spiritual journey.

The desire to be perceived as "good" or "divine" can indeed affect our experience of duality. When we seek to embody qualities that are traditionally associated with divinity or goodness, we may unintentionally create a sense of duality within ourselves. This duality arises from the contrast between our perceived ideal of goodness or divinity and the realities of our human nature and imperfections.

Perfectionism vs. Imperfection: The desire to be seen as good or divine may lead to striving for perfection. When we inevitably fall short of this ideal, we may experience a sense of duality between our perceived "higher" self and our "imperfect" self.

Judgment and Self-Criticism: A desire to be good and divine can lead to self-judgment and self-criticism when we believe we have not lived up to the expectations we set for ourselves. This internal judgment can create a duality between self-acceptance and self-rejection.

Denial of Shadow Aspects: In pursuit of goodness, we may suppress or deny our shadow aspects—the parts of ourselves we perceive as negative or undesirable. This duality emerges from the contrast between the "positive" aspects we embrace and the "negative" aspects we avoid.

Conditional Self-Love: The desire for goodness may lead to conditional self-love, where we only accept and love ourselves when we behave in alignment with our ideal. This creates a duality between self-love and self-rejection based on our actions and behaviors.

Comparison with Others: Seeking to be good or divine can lead to comparing ourselves with others who embody these qualities, perpetuating a sense of duality between ourselves and those we perceive as more spiritually advanced.

Spiritual Ego: The desire to be seen as good or divine can fuel the development of a spiritual ego, leading to a duality between the ego's need for validation and the desire for genuine spiritual growth.

Fear of Disapproval: The fear of not being seen as good or divine by others can create a duality between our authentic self-expression and the need for external validation.

To navigate this aspect of duality, it is essential to cultivate self-awareness and self-compassion. Embrace the full spectrum of your human experience, including both your light and shadow aspects. Recognize that the journey toward goodness and spiritual growth involves acknowledging and integrating all aspects of yourself. Allow yourself to be imperfect and understand that true divinity encompasses the entirety of the human experience. Embrace the process of growth and transformation with patience, love, and acceptance of yourself as a constantly evolving being on the path of spiritual exploration.

We cannot deny ourselves from human experience; by denying it we are unable to embrace and integrate the shadow.

Chapter 8: Cultivating Compassion

Learning to be gentle with ourselves as we navigate the complexities of our inner world: the mind, the spirit and the soul. Cultivating compassion is a crucial aspect of spiritual shadow work. It involves approaching your inner challenges, vulnerabilities, and hidden aspects with kindness, understanding, and non-judgment. Cultivating compassion for yourself during spiritual shadow work allows you to create a safe and nurturing environment for growth and healing. As you embrace your shadow aspects with love and understanding, you become better equipped to navigate the complexities of your inner landscape and step into a more authentic and empowered version of yourself.

Inner Child Work: Connect with your inner child—the vulnerable and innocent part of yourself. Offer love and care to this inner aspect that may have experienced pain or trauma.

Self-Reflection: Engage in regular self-reflection to understand the origins of your shadow aspects and the stories you tell yourself about them. This helps you develop empathy and compassion towards yourself.

Self-Compassion Affirmations: Use positive affirmations that emphasize self-compassion and self-acceptance. For example, repeat phrases like "I am worthy of love and understanding," or "I embrace all parts of myself with compassion."

Embrace Imperfection: Recognize that being imperfect is part of being human. Allow yourself to make mistakes and learn from them without harsh self-criticism.

Reframe Negative Thoughts: When negative or self-critical thoughts arise, reframe them with kinder, more understanding statements. Treat yourself as you would treat a dear friend going through a challenging time.

Boundaries and Self-Care: Set healthy boundaries in your life to protect your well-being and energy. Practice self-care activities that nourish your mind, body, and spirit.

Surrender Control: Recognize that not everything in life can be controlled or understood. Embrace uncertainty with grace and compassion towards yourself.

Forgiveness: Forgive yourself for past mistakes and perceived shortcomings. Understand that growth and healing involve learning and evolving from life's challenges.

Celebrate Progress: Acknowledge and celebrate your progress in your spiritual shadow work journey. Be gentle with yourself and remember that healing is a gradual process.

Cultivating compassion in spiritual shadow work is a profound act of self-love—a journey of embracing our totality and reclaiming our innate wholeness. Through the lens of compassion, we discover the beauty in our imperfections, the strength in vulnerability, and the profound wisdom within our shadows. As we tread this path with an open heart, we uncover the profound truth that the shadows are not to be feared but to be embraced with love, for they are the very steppingstones that lead us towards the luminous path of spiritual transformation and self-realization.

We need to understand what self-compassion is. The essence of self-compassion lies in treating ourselves with the same kindness, understanding, and care that we would offer to a dear friend who is suffering or facing challenges. It involves extending the same warmth and empathy to our own struggles, imperfections, and vulnerabilities, without harsh self-criticism or judgment. Self-compassion is a profound act of love and acceptance towards us, recognizing our shared humanity and inherent worth.

Key aspects of the essence of self-compassion include:

Kindness: Self-compassion starts with being gentle and kind to us, especially during difficult times or when we make mistakes. It involves offering ourselves words of comfort and encouragement, like a compassionate friend would.

Common Humanity: Self-compassion recognizes that suffering is a natural part of the human experience. It helps us understand that we are not alone in our struggles and that others, too, face challenges and imperfections.

Mindful Self-Awareness: Self-compassion requires a non-judgmental awareness of our thoughts, feelings, and experiences. We acknowledge and validate our emotions without getting overwhelmed by them.

Non-Self-Judgment: It involves letting go of self-judgment and self-criticism. Instead of berating ourselves for our flaws or failures, we respond with understanding and self-acceptance.

Self-Soothing: Self-compassion involves comforting ourselves during times of pain or difficulty. We offer ourselves a sense of warmth and soothing, providing emotional support.

Embracing Imperfections: Self-compassion acknowledges that no one is perfect, and we all make mistakes. It allows us to embrace our imperfections and understand that they do not define our self-worth.

Self-Forgiveness: Self-compassion includes forgiving ourselves for past mistakes and not dwelling on self-blame. It allows us to learn from our experiences and grow without unnecessary self-punishment.

Setting Boundaries: Self-compassion involves setting healthy boundaries to protect our well-being and prevent self-sacrifice for the sake of others.

Being Present with Ourselves: Self-compassion encourages us to be present with our emotions, both positive and negative, without trying to avoid or suppress them.

Cultivating Resilience: By treating ourselves with compassion, we foster resilience and a greater ability to navigate life's challenges with grace and strength.

The essence of self-compassion is a profound act of self-love and acceptance. By embracing our imperfections and offering ourselves understanding and care, we create a foundation of inner strength and compassion that ripples outward, positively impacting our relationships and interactions with others. Self-compassion allows us to hold ourselves with tenderness and become a supportive and nurturing presence in our own lives. It is a transformative practice that cultivates a deep sense of self-acceptance, well-being, and contentment.

Extending Compassion to Our Shadows

The Healing Power of Acknowledgment: We learn to acknowledge our shadows with compassion, understanding that denial only perpetuates their hold on us. Through acknowledgment, we release their grip on our lives.

Embracing the Inner Child: Compassion guides us to tenderly nurture our inner child, fostering healing and restoring the innocence that may have been wounded.

Mindful Witnessing: We practice mindful witnessing of our thoughts, emotions, and behaviors, offering ourselves compassion as we observe without judgment.

Compassionate Journaling: We explore the therapeutic practice of compassionate journaling, a sacred space where we pour our hearts onto paper with love and understanding.

Compassionate Communication: We learn to extend compassion in our interactions with others, fostering empathy and deep connection, while releasing judgment and criticism.

Boundaries and Compassion: We explore how setting healthy boundaries is an act of self-compassion, creating space for us to flourish in our relationships. Through compassion, we embrace the fullness of our being—the light and the shadow—with open hearts. As we walk hand in hand with compassion, we find liberation from the burdens of shame and judgment, opening the door to profound healing and transformation. With compassion as our constant companion, we transcend the limitations of our shadows, stepping into the radiant truth of our authentic selves. Embrace compassion as your gentle guide, and discover the limitless love that awaits within your soul.

The problem that most of us have is that we do not practice any kind of compassion or self-love. We are our worst critics and in the spectrum of shadow work this is an intricate part of the process.

Key aspects of the essence of self-compassion include:

Kindness: Self-compassion starts with being gentle and kind to us, especially during difficult times or when we make mistakes. It involves offering ourselves words of comfort and encouragement, like a compassionate friend would.

Common Humanity: Self-compassion recognizes that suffering is a natural part of the human experience. It helps us understand that we are not alone in our struggles and that others, too, face challenges and imperfections.

Mindful Self-Awareness: Self-compassion requires a non-judgmental awareness of our thoughts, feelings, and experiences. We acknowledge and validate our emotions without getting overwhelmed by them.

Non-Self-Judgment: It involves letting go of self-judgment and self-criticism. Instead of berating ourselves for our flaws or failures, we respond with understanding and self-acceptance.

Self-Soothing: Self-compassion involves comforting ourselves during times of pain or difficulty. We offer ourselves a sense of warmth and soothing, providing emotional support.

Embracing Imperfections: Self-compassion acknowledges that no one is perfect, and we all make mistakes. It allows us to embrace our imperfections and understand that they do not define our self-worth.

Self-Forgiveness: Self-compassion includes forgiving ourselves for past mistakes and not dwelling on self-blame. It allows us to learn from our experiences and grow without unnecessary self-punishment.

Setting Boundaries: Self-compassion involves setting healthy boundaries to protect our well-being and prevent self-sacrifice for the sake of others.

Being Present with Ourselves: Self-compassion encourages us to be present with our emotions, both positive and negative, without trying to avoid or suppress them.

Cultivating Resilience: By treating ourselves with compassion, we foster resilience and a greater ability to navigate life's challenges with grace and strength.

Chapter 9: Integrating the shadow

Embracing our wholeness by integrating the shadow aspect into the tapestry of the spirit of who we are in the moment of our existence. In the profound exploration of spiritual shadow work, we traverse the depths of our psyche, uncovering hidden aspects of ourselves—the shadows that lurk in the recesses of our consciousness. While confronting these shadows is essential for growth and healing, true transformation emerges through the integration of the shadow.

Understand that for this to happen you will need to accept the unwanted parts of who you are, the light and the dark, even those parts of yourself that you feel ashamed of. This is why the process of shadow work is one that needs Understanding, confrontation, embrace, transcendence, and compassion to be able to accept our duality without hurting ourselves. This entire process is one of self-realization and discovery to be able to integrate the shadows back where they belong. Those shadows are aspects of you and even though they may feel a separate entity they are extensions of you, they are you. By neglecting them you neglect yourself, by hurting them you hurt yourself. Love and accept the darkest aspects of you, this is part of integration and the only way you will experience wholeness.

Let's take the wolf as an example, the wolf cares for the pack, some nurture the pack and others lead the pack, but it is not in the nature of the wolf to be forgiving or to ignore what is needed for the pack and for the wolf. The nature of the wolf is to do what is necessary to be who the wolf needs to be. Is that evil? No, by embracing both light and dark and embracing who we truly are in this movement in time we integrate the shadow and even the unwanted parts.

How do we integrate the shadow? I will give you some examples that i'm sure you have heard before but with a small twist.

Rituals can provide a structured and sacred space for this work, helping us connect with our inner depths and embrace the hidden aspects of ourselves. Here are some rituals that can support the integration of our spiritual shadow self:

Cleansing Ritual: Begin by cleansing your physical space and yourself to create a sacred and energetically clear environment.

You can use smudging with sage or palo santo, take a purifying bath, or use essential oils to set the intention for the ritual.

Shadow Journaling: Set aside time to write in a special journal dedicated to your shadow work. Allow yourself to freely express your thoughts, emotions, and experiences related to your spiritual shadow self. Use this journal as a safe space to explore and understand your shadows.

Inner Dialogue Meditation: Practice a guided meditation or inner dialogue session where you engage in a conversation with your spiritual shadow self. Invite this aspect of yourself to speak to you, expressing its needs, fears, and desires. Respond with compassion and understanding.

Candle Meditation: Light a candle and sit in quiet meditation. As you focus on the flame, visualize your spiritual shadow self-coming to the surface. Embrace this aspect with love and acceptance, sending compassion towards it.

Elemental Release: Create a symbolic ritual using the four elements—earth, water, fire, and air—to release and integrate your spiritual shadow self. Write down aspects of your shadow on separate pieces of paper and then safely burn them (fire), bury them in the earth (earth), release them into flowing water (water), and let them be carried away by the wind (air).

Shadow Dance or Movement: Engage in a dance or movement practice that embodies the energy of your spiritual shadow self. Allow yourself to move freely, expressing the emotions and sensations associated with this aspect. As you dance, imagine integrating and transforming the shadow.

Oracle or Tarot Reading: Use oracle cards or a tarot deck to gain insights and guidance on your shadow integration journey. Draw cards with the intention of exploring your spiritual shadows and uncovering the lessons they hold for you.

Soul Collage: Create a soul collage representing your spiritual shadow self. Cut out images from magazines or printouts that resonate with this aspect of yourself and arrange them on a board or paper. Reflect on the meaning and symbolism of the collage.

Forgiveness and Releasing Ceremony: Write a letter of forgiveness to yourself, acknowledging any judgments or self-criticism related to your spiritual shadow self. Release these limiting beliefs by burning or tearing up the letter, symbolizing your willingness to let go and embrace compassion.

Integration Altar: Create a special altar dedicated to the integration of your spiritual shadow self. Place meaningful objects, crystals, and symbols representing your shadows on the altar. Use this space for meditation, reflection, and healing work.

I understand integration is not an easy process but worth it, it takes time to be able not to integrate but to accept who we truly are. This I would say is the hardest part of shadow work and integration. Now I want to also explain what happens when there is no integration, what are the consequences mundane and spiritual.

When we do not integrate the shadow, it can lead to various challenges and negative impacts on our well-being and personal growth. Here are some consequences of not integrating the shadow:

Repression and Denial: Unintegrated shadow aspects remain in the unconscious mind, leading to repression and denial. We may push away uncomfortable emotions, thoughts, or behaviors, avoiding dealing with them consciously.

Projection: Without integration, we are more likely to project our unacknowledged shadow aspects onto others. We may perceive and react to these aspects in others, which can lead to conflicts and strained relationships.

Emotional Repression: Unintegrated shadows can cause emotional repression, leading to a buildup of unresolved emotions. This can result in outbursts of anger, sadness, or anxiety that seem to come out of nowhere.

Self-Sabotage: Not integrating the shadow can lead to self-sabotaging behaviors, as we might unknowingly act out unresolved issues and patterns.

Spiritual Bypassing: Avoiding the shadow can lead to spiritual bypassing, where we use spiritual practices or beliefs as a way to avoid addressing deeper emotional or psychological issues.

Stagnation: Unresolved shadow aspects can hinder personal growth and development, keeping us stuck in repetitive patterns and preventing us from reaching our full potential.

Low Self-Esteem: Denying and suppressing parts of ourselves can lead to low self-esteem and a lack of self-acceptance, as we may judge ourselves harshly for having these aspects.

Disconnectedness: The unintegrated shadow can create a sense of disconnection within ourselves, as we are not fully in touch with all aspects of who we are.

Inner Conflict: Not integrating the shadow can create inner conflict, as we may struggle with contradictory thoughts, emotions, and desires.

Missed Opportunities for Growth: Each shadow aspect holds valuable lessons and opportunities for growth. By not integrating them, we miss out on the wisdom and insights they can offer.

Impact on Relationships: Unintegrated shadows can affect our relationships, leading to patterns of unhealthy dynamics or difficulties in connecting authentically with others.

Diminished Empathy: Lack of integration may reduce our ability to empathize with others, as we may not fully understand or acknowledge the complexities of human experiences.

Now what are some spiritual consequences when it comes to the shadow self-manifesting. One of them is a poltergeist, the energy of the shadow accumulates in your space and starts to manifest with noises, things moving or disappearing, even aggression towards someone or yourself. How would you feel if you were desperately crying for help desperately and no one cared? There will be a moment where you will have a reaction, this is what the shadow aspect of you does. Another form of manifestation is apparitions or shadows in your home. The shadow will always try to let you know in different ways that need help that needs integration. In my experience many times I have done a cleansing or an investigation instead of a spirit we have the manifestation of the shadow self. These spiritual manifestations can be confused with paranormal and spiritual activity. Cleansing and even banishments will not be effective if that is the case.

Integration is acceptance, self-love, looking at your shadow and you and saying we are one. We are light and darkness, we are the duality of us, we are the spirit of who we are but also the soul in its most primal aspect.

How do we know we have integrated the shadow?

Self-awareness: You are more aware of your thoughts, emotions, and behaviors, including the ones that were previously unconscious or denied. You can recognize when you are projecting your own unresolved issues onto others.

Embracing imperfections: You have become more accepting of your flaws and imperfections, understanding that they are a natural part of being human. You are less self-critical and judgmental of yourself and others.

Increased empathy and compassion: Integrating the shadow often leads to a greater understanding and empathy for others. As you accept and work through your own struggles, you become more understanding and compassionate towards the struggles of others.

Emotional balance: You experience a greater sense of emotional balance and stability. Instead of being overwhelmed or controlled by intense emotions, you can process them more effectively.

Authenticity: You feel more authentic and genuine in your interactions with others. You don't feel the need to hide or present a false image, and you can express your true self more freely.

Improved relationships: Integrating the shadow can lead to more fulfilling and harmonious relationships. As you become more aware of your own triggers and projections, you can relate to others in a healthier and more understanding way.

Integration of positive qualities: It's not just about acknowledging the negative aspects of the shadow self; it's also about recognizing and integrating positive qualities that were previously unrecognized or undervalued.

Acceptance of paradoxes: You become more comfortable with the contradictions within yourself and in life in general. You realize that life is not always black and white, and there can be value in holding conflicting emotions or ideas.

Less defensiveness: You are less defensive when receiving feedback or criticism, as you have a better understanding of your own strengths and weaknesses. You can view feedback as an opportunity for growth rather than a personal attack.

Sense of wholeness: Integrating the shadow self leads to a sense of inner wholeness and a feeling of being more in tune with your true self.

The moment of feeling complete, free, whole is the most amazing feeling as a spirit and a soul. The freedom to be you, the freedom to not feel judged by yourself, the freedom to be exposed to the world and nothing the world or society does affects you. That is true freedom, and I want all of you to experience it, to live it, to be you as you have always meant to be.

Final Though: Embrace the Depths: A Journey into Shadow Work"

In this book, we've embarked on a transformative odyssey, delving fearlessly into the uncharted territories of our psyche—the realm of the shadow. Together, we've explored the hidden corners of our souls, uncovering the veiled aspects of ourselves that once lurked in darkness.

As we bravely confronted our repressed emotions, desires, and vulnerabilities, we discovered that the shadow holds not just our fears, but also the seeds of our growth and liberation. Through introspection, compassion, and self-acceptance, we've learned to embrace the totality of who we are—flaws and all.

The journey of shadow work is not one of perfection, but of progress. It's about recognizing that true healing comes from acknowledging and integrating our shadow aspects, not suppressing or disowning them. We've harnessed the power of self-awareness to break free from the chains of projection, and in doing so, we've cultivated deeper connections with ourselves and others.

As we move forward, let us carry the torch of self-compassion to illuminate the paths of our fellow travelers. May this work serve as a guiding light for those seeking inner harmony, reminding them that the shadows we fear can become the stepping stones to our most authentic selves.

Remember, dear reader, to be gentle with yourself. The integration of the shadow is an ongoing journey—one that requires patience, courage, and resilience. Embrace your darkness with tenderness, for therein lies the beauty of your humanity.

As we close this chapter, let us embark on the next phase of our lives, equipped with newfound wisdom and self-empowerment. Embrace the depths of your being, for it is there that you will find the keys to unlock the doors of profound self-discovery and profound transformation.

May the shadows guide you toward the radiant light of your true self.

With love, acceptance and without judgment

Vlad Orfeo

Made in the USA
Monee, IL
07 November 2024

69614248R00079